Prohibition

Other titles in the American History series

AMERICAN HISTORY

Prohibition

John M. Dunn

LUCENT BOOKS
A part of Gale, Cengage Learning

GALE
CENGAGE Learning™

Detroit • New York • San Francisco • New Haven, Conn • Waterville, Maine • London

GALE
CENGAGE Learning

LIBRARY OF CONGRESS CATALOGING-IN-PUBLICATION DATA

Dunn, John M., 1949-
 Prohibition / by John M. Dunn.
   p. cm. -- (American history)
 Includes bibliographical references and index.
 ISBN 978-1-4205-0134-6 (hardcover)
 1. Prohibition--United States--History--Juvenile literature.
 2. Temperance--United States--History--Juvenile literature. I. Title.
 HV5089.D846 2010
 363.4'10973--dc22
                                                    2009032215

Lucent Books
27500 Drake Rd.
Farmington Hills, MI 48331

ISBN-13: 978-1-4205-0134-6
ISBN-10: 1-4205-0134-8

Printed in the United States of America
2 3 4 5 6 7 13 12 11 10

Printed by Bang Printing, Brainerd, MN, 2nd Ptg., 05/2010

Contents

Foreword

The United States has existed as a nation for just over 200 years. By comparison, Rome existed as a nation-state for more than 1000 years. Out of a few struggling British colonies, the United States developed relatively quickly into a world power whose policy decisions and culture have great influence on the world stage. What events and aspirations drove this young American nation to such great heights in such a short period of time? The answer lies in a close study of its varied and unique history. As James Baldwin once remarked, "American history is longer, larger, more various, more beautiful, and more terrible than anything anyone has ever said about it."

The basic facts of United States history—names, dates, places, battles, treaties, speeches, and acts of congress— fill countless textbooks. These facts, though essential to a thorough understanding of world events, are rarely compelling for students. More compelling are the stories in history, the experience of history.

Titles in this series explore history of a country and the experiences of Americans. What influences led the colonists to risk everything and break from Brit-ain? Who was the driving force behind the Constitution? Which factors led thousands of people to leave their homelands and settle in the United States? Questions like these do not have simple answers; by discussing them, however, we can view the past as a more real, interesting, and accessible place.

Students will find excellent tools for research and investigation in every title. Lucent Books' American History series provides not only facts, but also the analysis and context necessary for insightful critical thinking about history and about current events. Fully cited quotations from historical figures, eyewitnesses, letters, speeches, and writings bring vibrancy and authority to the text. Annotated bibliographies allow students to evaluate and locate sources for further investigation. Sidebars highlight important and interesting figures, events, or related primary source excerpts. Time-lines, maps, and full color images add another dimension of accessibility to the stories being told.

It has been said the past has a history of repeating itself, for good and ill. In these pages, students will learn a bit about both and, perhaps, better understand their own place in this world.

Important Dates at the

1775
The American Revolution begins.

1789
The French Revolution begins.

1822
First iron steamship makes its maiden voyage, traveling from England to Paris.

1840
Six reformed drinkers form the Washingtonian Movement in Baltimore, Maryland.

1839
The Opium War begins between Great Britain and China.

1775	1790	1805	1820	1835	1850

1785
Benjamin Rush publishes *An Inquiry into the Effect of Spirituous Liquours on the Human Body and Mind*.

1815
Napoléon Bonaparte's forces are defeated at Waterloo, ending his military power in Europe.

1826
The American Temperance Society is founded in Boston, Massachusetts.

1845
The Irish Great Potato Famine begins.

Time of Prohibition

1859
India officially becomes a British colony when the British government takes over control of the country from the British East India Company.

1914
World War I begins; it ends in 1918.

1920
Prohibition is enacted in the United States.

1925
A. Philip Randolph founds the Brotherhood of Sleeping Car Porters on May 8, the first national black labor union.

1893
The Anti-Saloon League forms in Ohio.

1920
William H. Stayton begins the Association Against the Prohibition Amendment (AAPA).

1929
On February 14, the St. Valentine's Day Massacre occurs in Chicago, Illinois, raising concern over crime in American cities.

| 1865 | 1880 | 1895 | 1910 | 1925 | 1940 |

1874
The Woman's Christian Temperance Union forms.

1923
Germany is shaken by a major economic crisis.

1930
Literary Digest, a popular weekly magazine, conducts a national survey that shows majorities in all but five states favor repealing Prohibition.

1933
Adolf Hitler and the Nazi Party take control of the German government. The Twenty-First Amendment repeals Prohibition in the United States.

1919
The Spanish influenza pandemic sweeps the world, killing over 30 million; Congress passes the Volstead Act.

1924
Ford Motor Company produces nearly 2 million Model-T cars.

The Noble Experiment

The crusade to ban alcohol in the United States lasted nearly a century, reaching its zenith in the 1920s. During that time, determined reformers exerted enough political power to convince a huge nation of millions to outlaw the commercial production and sale of intoxicating beverages enjoyed by millions of Americans for centuries. The earliest settlers in America sustained ancient beliefs that alcohol was a divine blessing that brought pleasure, cured disease, and gave fighting men courage.

These sentiments, along with the impact of war and a host of social and economic changes, helped create a nation awash in alcohol abuse by the nineteenth century. In 1810 an American adult drank 7 gallons of alcohol in a year on average. A decade later that number rose to 10 gallons per person. Although men were the heaviest drinkers, they were by no means alone in consuming alcohol.

The American Temperance Society, founded in Boston, Massachusetts, in 1826 to slow down consumption of alcohol in the United States, estimated that 9 million women and children drank 12 million gallons of distilled spirits year after year during the late 1820s. Three million men, meanwhile, consumed 60 million gallons annually.

This massive intake took its toll on Americans. Domestic abuse and abandoned families became widespread problems. Severe medical problems attributed to drinking were also common. Inebriation led many Americans to prison and early death. Drunkards, including preachers, politicians, and military leaders, roamed the alleys and fields. Upper-class Americans feared drunken mobs cause social disorder.

In response to these social ills, several outspoken Americans demanded the nation take another look at alcohol. A respected Revolutionary War hero and

An illustration showing the progression of a drunkard, demonstrating the toll alcohol takes on a man.

physician dared to suggest that, contrary to public opinion, distilled spirits did not promote human health; instead it was a poison and possibly addictive. Others claimed drunkenness stemmed from moral and religious failures.

At last an aroused citizenry decided to curb alcohol consumption. The majority of the new reformers sought only to temper (moderate) drinking habits by eliminating liquor, such as whisky or rum, but not beer or wine, which were less-potent fermented drinks. Some, however, wanted prohibition of all alcoholic beverages.

From the start, the clergy (church leaders) assumed leadership roles in the various regional temperance groups that formed in the country. And when medical facts failed to convince their audiences to become temperate (to limit their alcohol intake), the ministers appealed to human emotion and invoked biblical-based condemnation of alcohol. They railed against moral depravity caused by "strong drink" and predicted hellfire for the addicted, while turning the temperance movement into a religious crusade.

A nationwide temperance movement emerged during the early 1800s. As it passed through the nineteenth century, the crusade was shaped by wars, religious

The Shadow of Danger

**If you believe that the traffic in Alcohol
does more harm than good—** *help stop it!*"

Strengthen America Campaign

Strengthen America Campaign - 105 East Twenty Second Street, New York City, N.Y.

The temperance movement used the media, including posters like this, to show the dangers of drinking.

beliefs, tax concerns, immigration changes, changing norms and values, and public opinion that was influenced by newspapers, magazines, and other forms of mass media. By 1920 the temperance movement had transformed into something more powerful. It became a national struggle for the prohibition of alcohol, which had also become the law of the land.

To be sure, this first ever, nationwide ban pleased America's broad coalition of antialcohol forces. At first it did reduce drunkenness and alcohol consumption. However, the flaws in the new legislation quickly became apparent. Enforcing Prohibition proved to be extremely difficult, if not impossible. Realizing this, producers, sellers, and drinkers of alcohol flouted the law. Millions of Americans did their drinking secretly and purchased illegal whisky, rum, and beer from lawbreakers. Organized crime rushed to the lucrative alcohol black market that flourished during the heyday of Prohibition. Mobsters, eager to maximize profits from trafficking in illicit alcohol, slaughtered, intimidated, kidnapped, bribed, and terrorized anyone who got in their way.

As the shortcomings of Prohibition became apparent, a new national social movement emerged that sought to repeal the law. Critics were fed up with Prohibition. Many were weary of the crime and lawlessness. Some resented the national ban on liquor, because they considered it a violation of personal liberty. Other critics blamed Prohibition for contributing to an economic depression that had devastated the nation. A handful of Christians broke ranks from the majority of their faith and turned against Prohibition too. Judge Joseph F. Rutherford, the second president of the Watchtower Bible and Tract Society, argued in 1926 that Prohibition itself was corrupt and produced evil. As such, according to Rutherford, America's national antialcohol law was clearly the work of the devil. He said, "All Christians should refuse to stultify [deaden] themselves by joining hands with any scheme that has the appearance of good when in truth and in fact it is honey-combed with fraud and deceit, and denies the Lord and his method of accomplishing the blessing of mankind."[1] By the end of the 1920s, millions of average Americans, including those who had once supported temperance and prohibition efforts, now agreed that the nation's Noble Experiment had failed.

By 1932 America's political leadership responded to the change in public opinion. A new amendment to the U.S. Constitution effectively ended Prohibition. Once again the liquor trade was legal in the United States. With this reversal, however, the nation still had to contend with the consequences of a notorious beverage that, among other things, is the source of abuse, serious health problems, and contributes to the deaths of one hundred thousand Americans every year.

Chapter One

The Origins of Alcohol Abuse in America

The history of alcohol use in America began the day Europeans first arrived in the New World. Provisions aboard Christopher Columbus's sailing ships, the *Nina* and the *Pinta*, in 1492 included rations of two and a half liters of red wine per man. Ship officials believed that wine, along with other supposed benefits, relieved constipation. A little more than a century later, ships transporting English settlers to North America also carried tons of wooden barrels of beer on board. Not only did many passengers enjoy the taste of beer, but they also thought drinking it would prevent a disease called scurvy. At the time, this ailment was a common malady for sailors and others who went to sea for long periods of time and were deprived of fresh fruits and vegetables. Scientists later realized scurvy is caused by a lack of vitamin C.

Even the strictly religious Pilgrims, immigrants from England, transported so-called hot waters on the *Mayflower* to quench their thirst. In fact, they may have transported more beer than water to America. Water could not be relied on for drinking purposes, because it did not stay fresh during the weeks needed to cross the Atlantic Ocean. Alcoholic beverages, on the other hand, survived the long journey without spoiling.

Most of America's early colonists agreed that liquor was indispensable, especially in a strange land, where they planned to carve a civilization out of a wilderness. They, like so many other Europeans, held many old and cherished misconceptions about drinking alcohol. Among other things, these early immigrants considered alcohol literally a gift from heaven. Taken in modest amount, it was widely believed, liquor was one of life's blessings. Europeans were also convinced that alcoholic drinks were tonics that promoted good health that cured a variety of illnesses

Drinking was such a part of everyday life that laborers often took drink breaks during their workday.

and maladies, including frostbite, broken limbs, and malaria.

Breakfasts for all ages commonly started with a dram of cider, rum, whisky, or brandy. Colonists believed these drinks, or "bitters," provided vigor for the coming day. They also drank to keep warm in winter and to restore vital fluids when they sweated in summer.

Laborers enjoyed several drinking breaks during the workday during which they could drink a glass of grog supplied by employers who thought they were keeping their laborers strong and happy. Church bells sometimes rang to announce these liquor recesses. Even more drinking occurred in colonial homes at suppertime and afterward as colonists gathered to socialize at local taverns.

Colonists were also glad to have these beverages on hand because they could not always trust rivers, lakes, and other water sources in the American wilderness. As pioneers in a new land, they lived in primitive conditions and often lacked the means for purifying water and for keeping other drinks, such as milk, from becoming contaminated. For the most part, only rainwater and fresh water springs were thought to be safe for consumption, but even these sources were not always reliable or available. Moreover, many colonists believed that because water was tasteless and clear it lacked nutrients and other healthful ingredients. Drinks such as apple cider, on the other hand, seemed safer substitutes because they had strong flavor, color, and other features that were supposed to invigorate human life.

Colonists also used alcohol as a cure for external injuries. They dabbed pieces of cloth dampened with hard cider upon their skin, open sores, and other physical afflictions, expecting to be restored to good health.

Social Drinking in the Colonies

Alcohol's popularity, however, was not confined to the mistaken belief that it promoted good health and could be used a cure. Drinking alcohol was, in fact, a popular pastime in colonial America. Wherever colonists gathered, alcohol was sure to flow into cups, mugs, and glasses. Most social interaction took place at the local church and village taverns. Ministers and their congregations commonly met at taverns after religious services, where they drank, talked, and laughed for hours.

Children, meanwhile, learned to imitate their parents' drinking habits. In some households, parents taught their offspring to drink by giving them small amounts of alcohol. In this way, the adults believed their children would learn to drink responsibly and avoid alcoholism when they were older. Parents, however, were not the only adults who encouraged children to drink alcohol. According to Eric Burns, author of *The Spirits of America*,

> In some colonial schools, the books were put aside for a few minutes each morning and afternoon so that the children, who might not have gotten enough liquor upon awakening, could be given a few more tastes to revive their flagging attention. The teachers joined in just to be polite. The practice was considered as important a part of the classroom ritual as the rod and reader."[2]

Colonists, like these Puritans in Massachusetts, often gathered for social events at a tavern.

The demand for alcoholic beverages was so strong during America's prerevolutionary days that even farmland belonging to some churches was used to grow corn that was then turned into whisky, a distilled drink with a high percentage of alcohol. The Moravian churches of North Carolina produced not only whisky but also brandy, cider, and rum as well.

Despite its destructive, intoxicating effects, alcohol also played a big role in the lives of colonial fighting men. For centuries, American soldiers and sailors received daily rations of liquor, such as rum, even while they were on duty. Commanding officers believed these daily libations lifted the spirits of their men, gave them courage, and kept them fit and healthy.

Americans drank not only when they worked, but also when they visited friends and shopped at stores, where merchants provided liquor as refreshments. They also drank copiously at barn raisings, quilting bees, and weddings. Many even drank alcohol, often to the point of drunkenness, at funerals. Burns notes that during the colonial period,

men and women from all stations of life were laid to rest with portions of rum in their caskets, a little something to ease the passage from one world to the next. Even paupers were so equipped, the thought being that a few postmortem [after death] belts would give them hope that the afterlife would be a more congenial [agreeable] experience for them than the one so recently terminated."[3]

Early American courts often took breaks during legal proceedings so that attorneys, judges, and jurors could refresh themselves with swigs from a bottle of rum. Politicians routinely passed out free drinks on Election Day to curry favor with voters. Horace Greeley, a renowned nineteenth-century editor and political figure, was fully aware of the widespread use of alcohol. He said, "In my childhood there was no merry-making, there was no entertainment of relatives or friends, there was scarcely a casual gathering of two or three neighbors for an evening's social chat, without strong drink."[4]

A Former Slave Condemns Racism and Alcohol in America

In a speech to an audience in Paisley, Scotland, on March 30, 1846, Frederick Douglass, a famed author, orator, and former slave denounced the role of alcohol in the lives of American blacks. He said,

> Ladies and Gentlemen, I am proud to stand on this platform.... I have been excluded from the temperance movement in the United States, because God has given me a skin not coloured like yours. I can [verify] ... that the same spirits which make a white man drunk make a black man drunk too.... To give you [an idea] ... of this prejudice and passion against the coloured people, I may state that they formed themselves into a temperance procession in Philadelphia ... but they had not proceeded up two streets before they were attacked by a reckless mob, their procession broken up, their banners destroyed, their houses and churches burned, and all because they had dared to have a temperance procession.... They had saved enough to build a hall, besides their Churches. These were not saved, they were burned down, and the mob was backed up by the most respectable people in Philadelphia.... In the Southern States, masters induce their slaves to drink whisky ... to keep them from devising ways and means by which to obtain their freedom ... to ... make a man a slave, it is necessary to silence or drown his mind. It is not the flesh that objects to being bound—it is the spirit.

Frederick Douglass, *The Frederick Douglass Papers: Series One—Speeches, Debates, and Interviews*, vol. 1, eds. John W. Blassingame et al., New Haven, CT: Yale University Press, 1979, www.yale.edu/glc/archive/1118.htm.

Alcohol's Role in the Economy

Although some early European settlers had personal misgivings about alcohol use, few disagreed that manufacturing alcohol was a respectable way to make a living. Local governments commonly relied on the taxes and import dues they imposed on liquor to raise revenues. Among the most favored imports was rum, a drink produced in the West Indies that was distilled from molasses, a thick, dark-brown syrup made from sugar cane.

As demand for alcohol grew during the early 1700s, many New England merchants set up their own distilleries and manufactured rum themselves. Within a few decades, colonial companies were dispatching sailing ships loaded with barrels of rum to the west coast of Africa. Here, the cheaply produced American beverage replaced French brandy as a means of exchange and was used to obtain slaves. Next, the chained captives were transported to the West Indies in the Caribbean, where they were sold for molasses. Finally, molasses was shipped back to the American colonies to be used in the distillation process that produced rum.

In time rum was such a widely used product that its name became a generic term for all alcohol drinks in early America. Critics of drinking, however, coined the expression "Demon Rum" to characterize the damage caused by excessive drinking of any number of liquors.

Early Restrictions on Drinking

Despite their widespread spirit of permissiveness, colonial authorities, however, did set some limits on alcohol consumption. Although modest drinking was tolerated, alcohol abuse and drunkenness were not. The Puritans of Massachusetts, in fact, publicly whipped disgraced drunkards or forced them to wear a scarlet-colored letter D around their neck to publicly humiliate them, sometimes for as long as a year. Early Methodists, too, opposed excessive drinking. In 1672 Boston minister Increase Mather, the first president of Harvard University, explained this distinction in religious terms: "Drink is itself a good creature of God, and to be received with thankfulness, but the abuse of drink is from Satan, The wine is from God, but the Drunkard is from the Devil."[5]

In 1637 local lawmakers in Massachusetts enacted a rule to help remind citizens to be moderate in their drinking or face a fine. It read, "No person shall remain in any inn or victualing house, 'longer than necessary, upon payne of 20 Schillings for every offense'."[6]

Some communities, such as New Amsterdam, Providence Plantations, and other colonies, prohibited the sale of alcohol to American Indians who lived near white settlements. Alcoholic beverages, however, were not entirely new to Indians. Long before the arrival of Europeans, they had drunk fermented drinks made from fruits,

HENRY HUDSON OFFERING LIQUOR TO THE INDIANS ON THE NORTH RIVER.

British explorer Henry Hudson offering liquor to Native Americans. Several colonies, however, prohibited sale of alcohol to Indians.

ranging from berries to those of the giant cactus. Their traditional drinks, however, contained only a fraction of the alcohol found in the distilled alcoholic drink, also known as "ardent spirits," or "hard liquor" made by white settlers.

The desire to prevent Native Americans from drinking liquor did not arise from any concern about their health. Instead, it stemmed from a fear that drunken Native Americans posed a threat to colonists.

Drunken colonists, however, also created havoc. Now and then intoxicated white settlers, while seeking revenge or confiscating tribal lands, attacked and killed Indians. Such actions worsened ongoing hostilities between colonists and Native Americans and often led to bloodshed.

Georgia's Prohibition Experiment

Not all colonies made temperance their policy. The founder of Georgia, Englishman James Oglethorpe, wanted his colony to be alcohol-free. Oglethorpe, shocked by conditions in British jails and the lack of social justice for poor people, negotiated with King George II to allow him to relocate one hundred imprisoned British debtors to a colony on the southeast coast of North America where they could start their lives all over again.

View of James Oglethorpe

In this extract from a letter dated March 22, 1732 (or 1733), a visitor provides a sketch of Englishman James Oglethorpe, founder of the Georgia colony, before drinking became a problem at the colony:

> Mr. Oglethorpe is [untiring].... He is extremely well beloved by all the people. The general title they give him is Father. If any of them are sick, he immediately visits them, and takes a great deal of care of them. If any difference arises, he is the person that decides it.... He keeps a strict discipline. I never saw one of his people drunk, nor heard one of them swear, all the time I was there. He does not allow them rum; but in lieu gives them English beer. It is surprising to see how cheerful the men go to work, considering they have not been bred to it. There are no idlers there. Even the boys and girls do their part. There are four houses already up, but none finished; and he hopes, when he has got more sawyers ... to finish two houses a week. He has ploughed up some land; part of which he has sowed with wheat ... two or three gardens ... [and he is building a fort around the community] ... which I suppose may be finished in about a fortnight's time [two weeks]. In short, he has done a vast deal of work for the time; and I think his name justly deserves to be immortalized.

Quoted in Thaddeus Mason Harris, *Biographical Memorials of James Oglethorpe, Founder of the Colony of Georgia in North America*, Boston, MA: Freeman and Bolles, 1841, http://infomotions.com/etexts/gutenberg/dirs/1/0/6/7/10677/10677.htm.

At first Oglethorpe allowed the settlers to use small amounts of beer and molasses to sweeten livestock feed. To his great disappointment, the newly arrived Georgians instead used the molasses to make rum and soon drank themselves into a stupor. Infuriated by their behavior, Oglethorpe promoted the creation of the colony's London Trustees Act in 1735 to proclaim that "no Rum, Brandies, Spirits or Strong Waters"[7] could enter the colony. The act called for sellers of alcohol to be punished as lawbreakers and illegal alcohol confiscated and destroyed. Trustees hoped to impose a dose of morality on Georgians and to keep them sober so they could properly defend the borders and concentrate on building a prosperous colony. Georgia's authorities, however, soon found that it was hard, if not impossible, to enforce these restrictions. In fact, the manner in which the colonists reacted to this early attempt at prohibition provided a preview of the hardships America would experience when a national prohibition on selling, making, and consuming alcohol went into effect in the early twentieth century.

Corruption quickly surfaced as many Georgians and others outside the colony searched for ways to avoid the ban. Some colonial officials accepted bribes to look the other way, as smugglers sneaked in rum and whisky from other nearby colonies. Some Georgia settlers, meanwhile, set up their own illegal distilleries in remote areas of the colony, where they were hard to detect.

When efforts to catch and punish wrongdoers proved unsuccessful, scorn and ridicule erupted from colonists outside Georgia. At last, the trustees realized that America's first attempt at prohibition had failed and called it off in 1742. Among other concerns, they worried that the widespread flouting of an unpopular act would breed contempt for other rules and laws. Worse yet, the trustees recognized that prohibition benefited smugglers and rumrunners, instead of law-abiding colonists. And there was yet another reason—an economic one—for lifting the ban, according to historian Daniel J. Boorstin:

> Because timber was the most likely export of the colony, and its logical market was the sugar islands of the British West Indies which could send back little but rum in return, prohibiting the importation of rum was in effect of cutting off trade with the West Indies. This deprived the [British] empire of needed lumber and deprived the Georgians of profitable commerce.[8]

Rising Concerns

Lifting the ban on alcohol in Georgia, however, failed to end the debate on drinking alcohol in the thirteen colonies. Instead, concern was mounting over widespread reports of wife and child abuse and neglect, fights, injuries, idleness, drunkenness, and other social ills related to consumption of alcohol.

Increasingly, religious groups, such as the Quakers and the Methodists, spoke out against alcohol consumption. They argued that excessive drinking was not only destructive to human life, but also morally depraved and ungodly. Many church leaders argued that because drunkenness diverted people away from Christianity, it was a sin that had to be stopped.

Alcohol and the American Revolution

Arguments over alcohol, however, faded in 1775 when the armed colonists fought Great Britain to obtain their independence; this war became known as the American Revolution. Traditionally, colonial troops received a daily ration of a half-pint of rum to ward off winter chills and supplement meager rations of food. Rum was also expected to give them courage. Among those who often drank during wartime was George Washington, the general of the Continental army. Some historians point out, however, that Washington avoided drinking to excess and expected the same sort of restraint in his men. Nonetheless, General Marvin Kilman, a commander in the Continental army, once observed, "Much of George

General George Washington and his troops drank during the American Revolution thinking it would ward off chills and give courage.

Washington's continuing good cheer and famed fortitude during the long years of the war, caused to some extent by his overly cautious tactics, may have come from the bottle."[9]

Any impairment from drinking, however, did not stop Washington from leading his army, and the nation, to victory in 1781. Americans drank heartily to celebrate their new nation's independence, even long after hostilities had faded. After the war, some who had taken up arms in the name of independence drank to drown their wartime sorrows.

For many former soldiers, hard drinking with former comrades in a saloon became a way of continuing a brotherhood forged in battle. Such communal drinking may have also served as a way for common people to celebrate sentiments of equality that had once united them and helped fuel the war of independence.

Political figures running for elective office often drank with former soldiers to prove that they too believed in equality and democracy. Drinkers commonly "treated" or bought one another rounds of drinks in America's many taverns to show their friendship and hospitality. The main purpose at such gatherings, invariably, was to get drunk. "To be drunk was to be free," writes historian W.J. Rorabaugh. "The freedom that intoxication symbolized led Americans to feel that imbibing lustily was a fitting

Daily Drinking in the Continental Army

In his book, *1776*, author David McCullough provides this description of alcohol consumption among some American troops during the Revolutionary War:

> A British ship's surgeon who used the privileges of his profession to visit some of the rebel camps, described roads crowded with carts and wagons hauling mostly provisions, but also, he noted, inordinate quantities of rum—"for without New England rum, a New England army could not be kept together." The rebels, he calculated, were consuming a bottle a day per man.
>
> To judge by the diary of an officer with the Connecticut troops at Roxbury, Lieutenant Jabez Fitch, who enjoyed a social drink, there was considerably more besides plain rum to be had. "Drank some grog," he recorded at the close of one day, after a stop at a nearby tavern; "the gin sling passed very briskly," reads another entry. "In the morning I attended the alarm post as usual ... then down at Lt. Brewster's tent to drink Ens. Perkins' cherry rum, came back and eat breakfast." He imbibed wine and brandy sling, and on an expedition "up into Cambridge town," after a stop to sample "some flip" (a sweet, potent mix of liquor, beer, and sugar), he made for another tavern, the Punch Bowl, "where there was fiddling and dancing in great plenty ... I came home a little before daylight in."

David McCullough, *1776*, New York: Simon & Schuster, 2005, pp. 29–30.

way for independent men to celebrate their country's independence."[10]

But there was also widespread uncertainty over the new nation's experiment with self-government. American settlers were also expanding into the western reaches of North America and encountering Indian resistance. Anxieties also grew when the new nation was once again at war with Great Britain in 1812. Technological changes, along with steady immigration, brought about new economic and social conditions. All these factors contributed to an increase in public alcohol consumption. Much of it was binge drinking—that is, drinking to get drunk. "The changes in drinking patterns that occurred between 1790 and 1840 were more dramatic than any that occurred at any other time in American history,"[11] observes Rorabaugh.

The Whiskey Rebellion

The new republic faced many crises during its early days and one of them stemmed from a controversy over

A government inspector being tarred and feathered during the Whiskey Rebellion.

whisky. Following the end of the Revolutionary War, many farmers in western Pennsylvania found it cheaper and more profitable to convert corn and rye into alcohol and ship it to markets in the eastern part of the nation rather than to transport the bulky grain itself over long distances. Farmers, in fact, could expect about 25 cents for a bushel of corn; but that same bushel, if used to make whisky, could earn them four or five times that amount.

Meanwhile, the nation's first secretary of the treasury, Alexander Hamilton, had concluded that the nation needed to tax domestic whisky, a drink that was becoming increasingly popular with Americans. Hamilton argued that the levy was a good idea for several reasons. For one thing it would raise badly needed revenues for the federal government. He also argued that by waging the levy the new government could demonstrate its national power.

In addition, a levy on whisky would encourage Americans to reduce their intake of alcohol. As Hamilton pointed out in a 1790 report to Congress,

> the consumption of ardent spirits particularly, no doubt very much on account of their cheapness, is carried to an extreme, which is truly to be regretted, as well in regard to the health and the morals, as to the economy of the community. Should the increase of duties tend to a decrease of the consumption of those articles, the effect would be, in every respect desirable.[12]

That Hamilton—who limited himself to three drinks of wine every day—was seen by many as an advocate of moderation shows how deeply ingrained social drinking was in the country in the late eighteenth century.

Using these arguments, Hamilton convinced Congress in 1791 to impose a tax on imported liquor and all whisky produced in the country. This move, however, infuriated financially strapped

Pennsylvania farmers, who refused to pay the new tax. Their insubordination was significant, since many of the men were veterans of the American Revolution. They not only defied the U.S. government, but also tarred and feathered tax collectors and burned the stills of their neighbors who willingly paid the tax.

Alarmed at the growing Whiskey Rebellion, as it was now widely known, Hamilton persuaded Washington in 1794 to send fifteen thousand militiamen into western Pennsylvania to quell the uprising. Soon after the arrival of these federal troops, the rebelling farmers quickly dispersed. Cowed by the power of the new federal government, they also reluctantly paid the tax. Although the new tax enriched federal government coffers, it did little to suppress American thirst for rum and other intoxicating libations as Hamilton had predicted.

Hamilton, however, was not the only American to worry about the new nation's drinking habits. Across the new nation, others increasingly worried about the growing abuse of alcohol among their fellow citizens and rose up to stop what they believed was a national menace.

Chapter Two

The Temperance Movement Begins

Among those keeping vigil on America's drinking habits were members of the new nation's upper class. These watchdogs worried that an excess of public drunkenness could spark an uprising of the common people against those of privilege and wealth. Cracking down on public drinking seemed a sure way to keep their social inferiors in their places.

Other Americans, meanwhile, also wanted to curb drinking, but for different reasons. Their interest lay in protecting public health and moral character from the ravages of alcohol. Many thought the best way to do this was to act on the ideas of a former revolutionary. Unlike Washington, this American hero was an ardent critic and enemy of alcohol.

Benjamin Rush

Dispensing alcohol to men at war made no sense to Benjamin Rush, a signer of the Declaration of Independence, a member of Congress, the physician general of the Continental army, and the nation's first professor of medicine.

Rush had already developed moral qualms about alcohol before the American Revolution started. His experiences with soldiers wounded and killed in battle convinced him that, contrary to popular beliefs, alcohol was not good for the human body.

In 1778, after finding the living conditions of soldiers as deplorable, Rush published his pamphlet, *Directions for Preserving the Health of Soldiers*. In it he stressed to fellow officers the importance of cleanliness and good diet for their men. He also expressed his disagreement with the popular idea that consumption of rum protected American soldiers from the extremes of heat and cold. Rush argued instead that alcohol actually was the cause of many diseases that plagued soldiers. Although his published comments marked one of the first times that

Benjamin Rush published influential works stating that alcohol was not good for the human body.

the alleged benefits of alcohol had been questioned for nonreligious reasons, they were not yet fully developed and had little effect on army policy makers during the Revolution.

After the war ended, however, Rush gathered up what he had learned from his wartime experiences and published a more comprehensive and influential work—*An Inquiry into the Effect of Spirituous Liquors on the Human Body and Mind and Their Influence upon the Happiness of Society*, published in 1785. In this forty-page document, Rush, who was fascinated with the connection between the body and mind, used medical and non-medical reasons to attack heavy drinking of alcohol. Liquor had no food value, he wrote. When given to patients, it made their conditions worse. It caused

Rush Questions Army Rum Rations

Revolutionary figure and physician Benjamin Rush expressed misgivings about revolutionary soldiers receiving rations of alcohol in his pamphlet, *Directions for Preserving the Health of Soldiers, Addressed to the Officers of the Army of the United States.* In it he writes,

What shall I say to the custom of drinking spirituous liquors, which prevails so generally in our army? I am aware of the prejudices in favour of it…. The common apology for the use of rum in our army is, that it is necessary to guard against the effects of heat and cold. But I maintain, that in no case whatever, does rum abate the effects of either of them upon the constitution. On the contrary I believe it always increases them. The temporary elevation of spirits in summer, and the temporary generation of warmth in winter, produced by rum, always leave the body languid, and more liable to be affected with heat and cold afterwards. Happy would it be for our soldiers, if the evil ended here! The use of rum, by gradually wearing away the powers of the system, lays the foundation of fevers, fluxes, jaundices, and the most of diseases which occur in military hospitals. It is a vulgar error to suppose that the fatigue arising from violent exercise or hard labour is relieved by the use of spirituous liquors. The principles of animal life are the same in a horse as in a man; and horses, we find undergo the severest labour with no other liquor than cool water.

Benjamin Rush, *Directions for Preserving the Health of Soldiers, Addressed to the Officers of the Army of the United States*, Board of War, September 5, 1777, www.ncbi.nlm.nih.gov/books/bookres.fcgi/history/pdf_rush.pdf.

memory loss. Alcohol was also habit-forming and led to the deterioration of body and mind.

Rush included in his report a "moral thermometer," which was a chart that showed his imaginative view of the various vices, disease, and punishments drinkers could expect in their lifetime, depending on what they drank and how often. For instance, people who drank punch spiked with alcohol could expect "idleness, sickness" and to end up in "debt." But the fate of those who drank gin, brandy, and rum during the day and night was "murder, madness, despair"

and a likelihood of being hanged in the "gallows."[13]

Rush's Impact

Rush's forty-page booklet became popular. It sold 170,000 copies by 1815 and was reprinted for three decades, appearing in almanacs, newspapers, and periodicals. Businessmen, community leaders, professionals, and working people all read Rush's ideas. The pamphlet was excerpted, quoted, copied, and read across the American republic. It also captivated thousands of readers and helped to launch the nation's first temperance

A Temperance Society certificate from 1866, with a pledge to abstain from drinking.

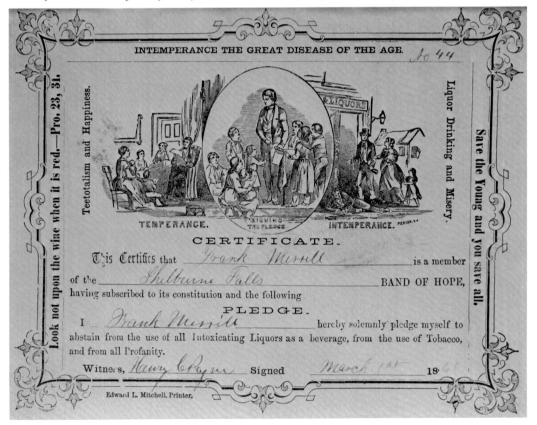

movement. Toward the end of his life, Rush hoped that the success of the movement would mean that by "1915 a drunkard ... will be as infamous in society as a liar or a thief, and the use of spirits as uncommon in families as a drink made of a solution of arsenic or a decoction of hemlock."[14]

Legions of Rush's readers took action. Many ministers stopped serving their congregations liquor. The Methodists and Presbyterian churches called upon their members to give up all alcoholic beverages. In 1789 the farmers of Litchfield, Connecticut, joined forces and forbid their employees from imbibing alcohol. Many factory owners also cracked down on employees who drank at work.

One of the leading antialcohol activists was Billy James Clark, a country doctor in upstate New York. Alarmed by what he read in Rush's pamphlet, Clark rushed to the home of a nearby minister and cried, "We shall all become a community of drunkards in this town unless something is done to arrest the progress of intemperance [excessive drinking]."[15] Next, Clark invited a small group of like-minded men to a meeting at a local schoolhouse on April 30, 1808. There they formed the Union Temperance Society of Moreau and Northumberland. Its members pledged to stop drinking distilled alcohol on a trial basis for a year and hoped that others would follow their example.

News of Clark's group spread and soon many similar temperance groups appeared in New York, New England, and the Midwest. The largest of these became known as the American Temperance Society, an organization that vowed to close down the nation's four thousand distilleries. Founded in 1826 in Boston, Massachusetts, the organization soon boasted five thousand local chapters and a membership of about 1 million spread across the country. Many of the members publicly pledged to moderate their use of alcohol at temperance revival meetings. Others vowed to abstain from all alcohol altogether. The letters "TA" were written next to the names of these "total abstainers" on membership rosters. Since the "T" stood for "total," this practice gave rise to the term *teetotaler*, which is still in use today to describe a person who does not drink alcohol.

The Virginia Temperance Society appeared a few months later, becoming the first major temperance organization in the South. Other similar groups soon formed in the southern states; however, the early temperance movement in the South was never as strong as it was in the North. One reason for the lack of support was that many white southerners were hesitant to support a movement, whose northern members were likely to also support the abolition of slavery—a practice that provided the economic foundation for southern states.

A Variety of Approaches

Within a few years, approximately five thousand antidrinking societies had formed in the United States with a wide range of temperance goals. Some wanted to close all distilleries and drinking establishments. Others sympathized with drunkards and tried to redeem them. This approach seemed a waste of time to some reformers, who believed it made more sense to concentrate on convincing moderate and nondrinkers to shun liquor, or at least drink only beer and wine instead. More radical temperance activists, however, insisted that the only liquid worth drinking was water that was both pure and cold. It was, they said, unpolluted and healthful.

Another approach was to appeal to a sense of patriotism. Author Eric Burns sums up a common question often posed by temperance volunteers: "What sense does it make for us to have won our independence from King George III [during the America Revolution] when we have become … [obedient] … instead to the bottled … [temptations] of the devil?"[16]

Few temperance groups sought new laws to moderate or ban alcohol at this point of the movement's history. Instead, antialcohol forces usually relied on the power of persuasion and education to change human behavior. Proponents of this approach believed individuals should make up their own minds about drinking. Many pointed to Oglethorpe's failure to ban alcohol in Georgia as a reminder that outlawing a human behavior was unlikely to work.

In addition to temperance organizations, various alcohol-free hotels and steamboats sprang up across the country. There were even temperance communities and towns, such as Harvey, Illinois, which was originally intended for residents seeking Christian values and an alcohol-abstaining way of life.

An Appeal to the Emotions

As the temperance movement grew, many activists learned that using the somewhat scientific approach of Rush was not as convincing as an appeal to the emotions. Many reformers now also quoted the words of Reverend Lyman Beecher, a pastor in Litchfield, Connecticut, who in 1825 published a collection of his fiery antidrinking sermons in a book titled, *Six Sermons on the Nature, Occasions, Signs, Evils and Remedy of Intemperance*. Beecher argued that alcohol damaged the physical, mental, and spiritual health of the individual. In his book he writes,

Whoever, to sustain the body, or invigorate the mind, or cheer the heart, applies habitually the stimulus of ardent spirits, does violence to the laws of his nature, puts the whole system into disorder…. The effect of ardent spirits on the brain, and the members of the body, is among the last effects of intemperance, and the least destructive part of the sin. It is the moral ruin which it works in the soul, that gives it the denomination of giant-wickedness.[17]

These religious lectures hit a nerve across America. Clergy everywhere proclaimed Beecher's words from the pulpit. They were reprinted in books and periodicals for more than a decade and eventually became the core text for the

A cartoon showing the temperance movement's belief that alcohol brings terrible things, including murder and disease.

next phase of the temperance movement. Some historians, in fact, believe that Beecher's book proved more influential than Benjamin Rush's 40-page booklet.

Soon, in villages, towns, and cities, church leaders and other public antialcohol speakers held crowds spellbound with lurid tales that focused on the perils and evils of drinking. Factual explanations often evolved into exaggerations and wild claims. Alcohol, for instance, was said to be the drink of the devil. James B. Finley, a Methodist circuit rider claimed, "I never knew a man who was in the habit of drinking regularly that did not become a drunkard."[18] Speakers

enthralled audiences with tales of drunkards whose blood was so seeped in alcohol that they suddenly burst into flames. Although hard to verify, accounts of these occurrences of spontaneous combustion bloomed across the new nation.

In addition, temperance writers produced a bounty of brochures, articles, novels, songs, and plays that portrayed lurid accounts of drunkards who abused and neglected their loved ones.

Another outspoken and influential clergyman was Boston's Reverend Justin Edwards, who eventually expanded a sermon into a "Temperance Manual" that was read across America in the 1830s.

Spontaneous Combustion

Minister W.R.G. Mellen of the Unitarian Church in Dover, New Hampshire, hoped to discourage his congregation from drinking when he gave the following sermon on March 19, 1882:

A young man, about twenty-five years of age … and a habitual drinker for many years. I saw him about nine o'clock in the evening on which it happened. He was … as usual, not drunk, but full of liquor. About eleven the same evening I was called to see him. I found him literally roasted from the crown of his head to the soles of his feet. He was found in a blacksmith's shop just across the way from where he had been. The owner all of the sudden discovered an extensive light in his shop as though the whole building was in one general flame. He ran … and on flinging open the door discovered a man standing erect in the midst of a widely extended silver-colored blaze, bearing, as he described it, exactly the appearance of the wick of a burning candle in the midst of its own flame. He seized him by the shoulder & jerked him to the door, upon which the flame was instantly extinguished.

There was no fire in the shop, neither was there any possibility of fire having been communicated to him from any external source. It was purely a case of spontaneous ignition.

W.R.G. Mellen, "The Moral Condition of Dover," sermon delivered in the Unitarian Church, March 19, 1882, Dover Public Library, www.dover.lib.nh.us/DoverHistory/temperance.htm.

Edwards rejected the centuries-old idea that liquor was a pleasure given from God. Instead, he argued, such a notion was as different from God's life-affirming creation as "poison is from food, sickness from health, drunkenness from sobriety."[19]

Edwards also dismissed the idea that moderate drinking did no harm. Alcohol, he argued, inflicted a host of injuries on the human body. According to him, it caused black ulcers and cancers to form inside a person. A drinker "cannot digest his food," he wrote. "The system is not nourished. Other organs become diseased, till the body itself is literally little else than a mass of putrefaction."[20] Edwards added that people would live longer and lead more productive lives if they abstained from alcohol altogether.

Religious Views on Alcohol

The growing religious and moral tone used by temperance workers produced considerable debate among churches and religious groups. Many of their leaders argued that drunkenness was proof of

People drinking and dancing in a tavern, a place church leaders spoke out against.

humanity's fall from the grace of God. Alcoholics and drunks were viewed by many as lapsed Christians, if not infidels, whose souls were doomed for eternity unless they reformed. In 1812 Reverend Heman Humphrey proclaimed, "Intemperate drinking is the highway to perdition ... a fiery stream which empties into a bottomless pit. All who ... embark on this flood are in danger of hell fire."[21]

Although many church leaders drank alcohol during colonial times, a growing number were abstaining by the early nineteenth century and spoke out against the growing "social evil" of drunkenness. From their pulpits many ministers preached that alcohol led too many young people to prostitution, crime, prison, and poverty. Worst of all, the religious leaders said, it caused many men to abuse their wives and children and squander family resources on drunkenness.

Scorn was also heaped upon the controversial businesses that sold alcohol, especially the saloons. According to Reverend Mark Matthews of Seattle, Washington's First Presbyterian Church, "the saloon is the most fiendish, corrupt, hell-soaked institution that ever crawled out of the slime of the eternal pit."[22]

Although there was widespread agreement among America's religious leaders over the bad effects of alcohol, they differed over what the Christian Bible said about drinking. Their disagreement stemmed from the fact that the holy book contains contradictory passages on the subject. Some say wine is a blessing. Elsewhere are warnings against alcohol abuse. There is also scripture that insists on abstinence. Since Jesus drank wine, some Christians insisted that the wine mentioned in the Bible must be grape juice, a view some scholars call ridiculous.

Searching for a National Policy

As the mid-1800s approached, reformers across the country realized the need to band together and work with a single purpose to lessen the impact of drinking on American society. But they could not agree on what their goals and tactics should be. Those favoring temperance still favored using moral persuasion, including the use of biblical scripture and public shame, to convince their fellow citizens to avoid alcoholic drinks. Other activists, meanwhile, wanted to pressure lawmakers to ban distilled liquor, if not all alcoholic drinks. Reformers also disagreed over whether a national movement should ignore drunkards and instead focus on the task of convincing moderate drinkers to give up drinking before they became addicted. Or, should they make the producers and sellers of alcohol their primary targets?

Eventually, these debates caused disunity. And as they continued, many reformers feared that the temperance movement was in danger of losing its momentum.

New Converts and Crusaders

The reformers' fears proved premature. In fact, the antialcohol struggle soon received a boost thanks to the work of six men who were heavy drinkers at Chase's Tavern in Baltimore, Maryland. On the night of April 2, 1840, two of the men attended a temperance lecture held elsewhere in the city, expecting to be amused. Instead, they found themselves captivated and converted by the speaker, Reverend Matthew Hale Smith of New York.

Transformed by the clergyman's message, the two men renounced liquor. Next, they convinced their drinking partners to do the same. Then, the six converts, along with other reformed drinkers, formed the Washington Temperance Society of Baltimore and hosted weekly meetings to convince drunkards to give up drinking and lead more wholesome lives.

At the meetings—perhaps foreshadowing the modern Alcoholics Anonymous organization—former drunks stood before their peers to relate personal stories of how alcohol had ruined their lives. They added testimonials of how they had also triumphed over drink. Many speakers even told tales of grappling with the devil who had tempted and ruined them. Often during these sessions, speakers would point to a shabby drunkard on stage who had been hired off the street as a living example of the rampages of drinking. Hundreds of curious people in the Baltimore area soon flocked to the meetings, where speakers emphasized experience and inspiration, rather than religious condemnation, to a curious public.

Women and Children Join the Fight

At first the Washington Temperance Society of Baltimore limited membership

A Song of the Cold Water Army

In the 1850s, members of the Cold Water Army sang lyrics, such as these:

'Tis my delight of a shiny night

Did you ever hear of the Army
The Washingtonians form?
Did you ever hear of the citadel
Of Alcohol's they storm?

O! it is a conquest glorious;
Come, spread the tidings wide;

O! we'll sing a song victorious,
And join their ranks beside.

Long has he checked his enemies,
And held them all at bay;
But now the Washingtonians
Big fair to win the day.

O! it is a conquest, &c.

Quoted in R.K. Potter, ed., *The Boston Temperance Songster; A Collection of Songs and Hymns for Temperance Societies. Original and Selected*, Boston, MA: White and Potter, 1846, http://lincoln.lib.niu.edu/cgi-bin/philologic/getobject.pl?c.1066:1.lincoln.

to alcoholics, but later admitted others. Soon chapters formed across the nation, attracting hundreds of thousands of new members. On May 12, 1841, a women's version of the movement called the Martha Washingtonians also was formed in New York. The goal of this early women's temperance movement was to focus on the abuse and hardship that women and children suffered at the hands of alcoholic men. The Martha Washingtonians took part in parades, as men heckled and booed from the sidewalks.

The women also hired professional speakers to spread their message that alcohol was akin to evil and that cold clean water was the best thing a person could drink. Author Lorenzo D. Johnson observed some of the New York activists and wrote,

You will find their visiting committees going most frequently "two and two," like the Apostles of old, looking into the dark corners of our towns and cities, into the damp cellars and open garrets, to find those whose poverty and suffering they can control, by pointing out to them a more excellent way of living, and encouraging them to walk in it, by offering them pecuniary aid [money]."[23]

Americans also saw the emergence of a temperance organization for children called the Cold Water Army. It was founded by Thomas P. Hunt, a Presbyterian minister, who believed that temperance energies were better spent teaching children to avoid the dangers of alcohol rather than trying to help hard-to-reform adult drunks. In Cold Water Army chapters across the country, children pledged to drink cold water instead of alcohol and marched through busy city streets, waving banners and singing temperance songs.

A Change in Approach

By the 1850s, the Washington Temperance Society had exhausted itself. But other popular groups took its place, such as the two hundred thousand strong Orders of the Sons of Temperance, Orders of Templar of Honor and Temperance, the Independent Order of Good Templars, and other similar organizations. According to author J.C. Furnas, these groups took on the characteristics of fraternal orders. Furnas writes, "All had secret meetings under guard, grips, passwords, officers' titles ... [and civic parades in which members marched] ... sweatily under their gaudily embroidered trappings of mystic meaning, the band playing some such Temperance

A group from the Independent Order of the Good Templars.

war song as 'Away the Bowl!'" or members would sing,

No matter what anyone says, no matter what anyone thinks.

If you want to be happy the rest of your life

Don't marry a man if he drinks![24]

Making Prohibition the Law

Despite the efforts of these organizations, Americans continued to drink vast amounts of alcohol. Convinced that neither persuasion nor an appeal to emotion and religion had done much to sway most American drinkers, many reformers now clamored for tougher measures. In fact a growing number of activists now wanted the very thing many early temperance workers had hoped to avoid. That is, they sought new laws that would criminalize drinking.

Supporters of the new emphasis on legal action were buoyed by an 1847 U.S. Supreme Court decision that held that the nation's Constitution did not forbid state governments from regulating or banning the sale of liquor. This judicial decision came as a blow to the group of liquor dealers who had filed the original lawsuit, hoping that a more favorable court ruling would discourage prohibition attempts at the state level.

Many reformers, though, were delighted with the ruling. Once again, however, disagreements over how to proceed flared up among the ranks of the antialcohol forces. Some of the new hardliners wanted to work for the passage of laws that allowed local governments to restrict or ban the issuing of new liquor licenses to businesses. Others argued that legislation was needed that forbid the drinking, manufacturing, or sale of only hard liquor, or all intoxicating beverages.

Tough Laws in Maine

As reformers in different states went to work lobbying local and state lawmakers to pass some kind of antialcohol laws, they found themselves following legal precedents already in place. Some states had already experimented with making alcohol illegal at the start of the temperance movement. Maine, for instance, was one of the first states to restrict liquor sales. In 1820, for example, state lawmakers authorized "whipping for those who sold 'strong water' without a license."[25] A year later, new legislation was passed that required that the "names of persons reputed [to be] common drunkards or common tipplers were to be posted by selectmen in all licensed places, and liquors were not be furnished to such."[26] In addition anyone thought to be "idle" or given to "excessive drinking" could be prohibited from purchasing liquor for a year.

In 1838 Maine prohibited sales of alcohol in amounts less than 15 gallons. The intent of this action was to discourage alcohol consumers by forcing them to pay dearly each time they made a purchase. Transporting such a large quantity of liquor was also expected to discourage purchase. Instead, determined drinkers pooled their money together and shared the labor of carrying the liquor away. Some customers bought the required 15 gallons, along with a single glass of rum or whiskey. After swallowing the drink, they returned the 15 gallons and asked for their money back, which the merchant was usually glad to provide.

Frustrated lawmakers repealed the law two years later, but also passed a new one allowing local governments to ban alcohol. This was not enough regulation, however, for a feisty Quaker named Neal Dow in Portland, Maine. An avowed enemy of alcohol, Dow was determined to make prohibition, not temperance, the law of his native state.

Neal Dow

A short, dapper man with steely eyes and dark curly hair, Neal Dow had retired early in life from a successful business career in timber, tanning animal hides, and banking. Afterward, Dow served briefly as Portland's fire chief. One day, according to some accounts, he reportedly ordered his fire crew not to extinguish a fire that was devouring a liquor store. Although Dow denied this version of events, the story nonetheless bolstered his reputation as a stern crusader for prohibition. Dow soon quit the fire department and formed the Maine Temperance Union. Determined to make prohibition a statewide issue, he personally traveled thousands of miles in Maine, conducting a door-to-door campaign to urge forty thousand citizens to sign an antialcohol petition. He also encouraged them to vote for prohibitionist candidates for political office, regardless of party affiliation.

In 1846 thanks in great measure to the influence of Dow's growing political power, the Maine legislature outlawed alcohol across the state. However, the new law was riddled with loopholes. Worse yet, Maine's antiprohibition governor, John Dana, vetoed a companion bill in 1849 that required state officials to enforce the prohibition law. Instead, enforcement was left in the hands of local authorities.

Maine's political landscape, however, changed during the next few years and by 1850 prohibitionists controlled the state legislature. A year later, they passed

Neal Dow formed the Maine Temperance Union and went door-to-door to campaign against alcohol.

a new statewide prohibition law—one designed by Dow himself—that banned the sale of alcoholic beverages. They also imposed a tough enforcement policy that included search-and-seizure raids, fines, and imprisonment. This meant that local authorities now had the legal right to confiscate and destroy any bottled spirits they found. They were also empowered to close down drinking establishments. At last, Maine had become the first state to go "dry."

As Maine Goes, So Goes the Nation

The Maine law caused controversy across the nation. Many supporters agreed with Reverend Lyman Beecher's assessment of what had happened in Maine. "God's work every step of the way … the pavers of hell are in dismay,"[27] as he told his congregation.

Critics, however, were appalled by Dow's ongoing liquor raids and called supporters of the law "Maine-iacs." They mocked Dow's high-handed methods, referring to him as the "Napoleon of Temperance." Undeterred by these verbal attacks, Dow called upon the rest of the nation to follow Maine's lead. In fact, the expression, "as Maine goes, so goes the nation," may have come from the fact that many states did follow. In 1852 Vermont, Massachusetts, Rhode Island, Oregon, and Minnesota passed their own "Maine" laws. Connecticut took action in 1854, and by 1855 Indiana, Delaware, Nebraska, Michigan, Pennsylvania, New York, and New Hampshire had passed their own versions of prohibition laws. In addition, prohibition bills had been narrowly defeated in several other states.

Getting Around the Law

Enforcing the new prohibition laws, however, proved much harder than passing them. Many residents in Maine, for instance, quickly found ways to take advantage of loopholes in the new state law. For one thing, smugglers found they could easily transport rum into Maine from neighboring states. In addition some unethical doctors prescribed alcohol as medicine for patients willing to pay them a fee. Many residents also sidestepped the law by purchasing liquor through the postal system, another legal loophole. Lawmakers themselves weakened the new prohibition law by amending it to allow hotels to sell rum.

Worse yet for the proponents of prohibition, a rum riot broke out in Portland, Maine, on June 2, 1855. The incident was sparked by a rumor that Dow, now the mayor of Portland, had stashed a private hoard of alcohol in City Hall. What he had stored in the building was a legal shipment of medicinal alcohol, but this fact was not known, or was ignored, by his enemies who descended as an angry mob upon City Hall. Many of the protesters were Irish immigrants, who complained that prohibition was a deliberate ethnic slur directed at their alcohol-imbibing culture. When the mob got out of hand, the governor called out the local militia and Dow himself gave the order to fire.

MAINE LIQUOR LAW—BURNING EFFIGIES OF GOVERNMENT OFFICERS AT ST. JOHNS, NEW BRUNSWICK.

During the Rum Riot in Portland, Maine, the local militia opened fire on the crowd.

When the shooting stopped, one sailor lay dead, and many others were wounded.

Maine was not the only state to see its attempt to criminalize alcohol falter. Similar troubles also emerged in the other states that had followed Maine's example. In the coming decades, many of the new antialcohol laws would be repealed, or came to an end, in the wake of various legal challenges or revocation by state governments.

The failure of the state prohibition laws also had left many Americans wondering if banning alcohol was a worthy goal. Many now agreed with Abraham Lincoln, who in 1840 reportedly told his fellow representatives in Illinois state legislature that "prohibition goes beyond the bounds of reason in that it attempts to control a man's appetite by legislation and makes crimes out of things that are not crimes."[28]

The Nation Focuses on War

As the 1860s began, all questions of temperance and prohibition were being overshadowed by a national crisis. After decades of animosity, the northern and southern states had become bitterly divided over slavery and other political and economic issues. In 1861 rebel troops fired on Fort Sumter at Charleston, South Carolina, igniting a catastrophic civil war. The survival of the nation was now at stake, and concerns about alcohol faded, as Americans focused on war.

The temperance movement was also derailed when the U.S. Congress passed the Internal Revenue Act in 1862. Signed into law by President Abraham Lincoln, the law was designed to finance the Union war effort, by imposing the nation's first graduated income tax, along with other revenue-raising measures, including a fee on the production of liquor, ale, and beer.

At first, temperance advocates celebrated the new tax, thinking it would reduce alcohol consumption. However, writes Burns, "the armies of abstention should have been the leading foes of the new monies, fuming and fussing rather than voicing their support, because what the taxes did, for the first time, was make the liquor industry an important part of the American economy."[29]

Although many Americans expected the tax to expire when the war ended, it continued for decades afterward. Politicians and citizens alike became accustomed to the revenues it provided the federal government. Some government officials even hoped for increased liquor sales to provide even more government funding. Thus, proponents of temperance found it hard to advance their cause when the war ended in 1865.

The Civil War took a toll on the temperance movement in yet other ways. No new state prohibition laws were passed between 1856 and 1879. The states that had passed them in the early 1850s paid scant attention to enforcing them during the war and the Reconstruction years.

However, new drinking problems emerged in the postwar period, as many disillusioned soldiers returned home and turned to alcohol to escape the trauma of their experiences at war. During the postwar period, America also became more urbanized, as displaced farmers and rural residents moved to cities to find work. Here they found low pay and squalid living and working conditions that drove many people to saloons to drink away their woes.

Once again the nation focused on issues of poverty, crime, drunkenness, and abuse. Meanwhile, a new political power was building up steam across the nation that demanded to be heard. It was the organized strength of American women.

Chapter Three

Women's Crusade Against Demon Rum

American women had been considered inferior to men and treated as second-class citizens since colonial times. Following the Civil War, they could not vote in most states. Most professional jobs were forbidden to them. In addition, they lost all rights to their own property when they married. Public expectations were that they find contentment in tending to the affairs of family and home.

American law had also suppressed women. Part of their burden stemmed from the legal practice known as coverture, which persisted in the country until the mid-nineteenth century. Scholar Carol Mattingly explains how it worked, "When women married, their personal property, and to differing extents their real property, their persons, their labor, and their children came under the ownerships of the husbands."[30] And all too often, many women and children were also expected to silently endure the abuse of alcoholic husbands.

Women who defied these customary attitudes and spoke out publicly on the issue were viewed as unseemly and unfeminine. On March 1852, for example, women temperance activists were denied the opportunity to speak at the New York meeting of the Sons of Temperance in Albany, New York. The organization's president told them they could only listen. A year later, cries of "shame on woman"[31] filled the meeting hall, as jeering men prevented Antoinette Brown from speaking at the World's Temperance Convention in New York City.

Diocletian Lewis

Such traditional attitudes, however, were soon challenged by a nationwide women's crusade to revitalize the temperance movement. It was a man, however, that helped to spark the movement. He was Diocletian Lewis, a self-proclaimed

Protect the Children

Speaking at the 1853 World Temperance Convention, temperance activist Antoinette Brown implored her audience to protect children from the abuses of drunkenness with these words:

> Look at their degradation, when they are cursed with drunken parents. Look now in this dear little face. It would be fair enough, if there were only a soul-life to flash over it. But it is an almost blank vacuity. You read there impressions of a gross nature, notwithstanding all that baby innocence. Yet you see a shadow over that face, reflecting the past and prophetic of the future. Poor child; with that worn little face smothered with dirt and filth. Fit emblem of your life is the little mole that lives under ground. There is sunshine in the sky, but you will never look upward. You may bow your head, for your one talent is rolled up in the napkin of parental sin. God of justice, must there be every year thousands of such children born in or land? ... Here is another child, with baby smiles and baby tears crossing each other down its face, gushing up from its little heart-fountain, struggling each for the mastery. If God would only take her to Heaven now, she would become one of the happiest of angel cherubs; but the fevered effect of the wine-cup delirium descends through her face, and the angels will weep over her, and remorse will pluck out the smiles....

Carol Mattingly, *Well-Tempered Women: Nineteenth Century Temperance Rhetoric*, Carbondale: Southern Illinois University Press, 1998, p. 32.

doctor, writer, public speaker, and promoter of physical fitness. A dashing figure with flowing white hair and dazzling blue eyes, Lewis discovered while making a speech in 1873 that he could enthrall audiences with a boyhood story of a band of church women that had once closed saloons in his small town by singing and praying.

One of the women swayed by Lewis's story was Eliza J. Thompson of Hillsboro, Ohio, a town of five thousand residents. A gentle, reserved woman in her sixties, Thompson believed she had received a spiritual calling to protest the presence of alcohol in Hillsboro, which, despite being a small, conservative, religious community, had thirteen saloons and eight other businesses that sold alcohol. Gathering one hundred like-minded women to her cause, Thompson led a march through the town. The women descended upon the local drinking establishments, sang hymns, prayed, and quoted Bible verses in an effort to rid the town of liquor. Shamed and embarrassed, the owners of all twenty-one establishments closed their businesses.

VOL. IV.   All the News. Four Editions Daily.   NEW YORK, THURSDAY, MARCH 5, 1874.---TRIPLE SHEET. $13 Per Year in Advance. Single Copies, Five Cents.   NO.

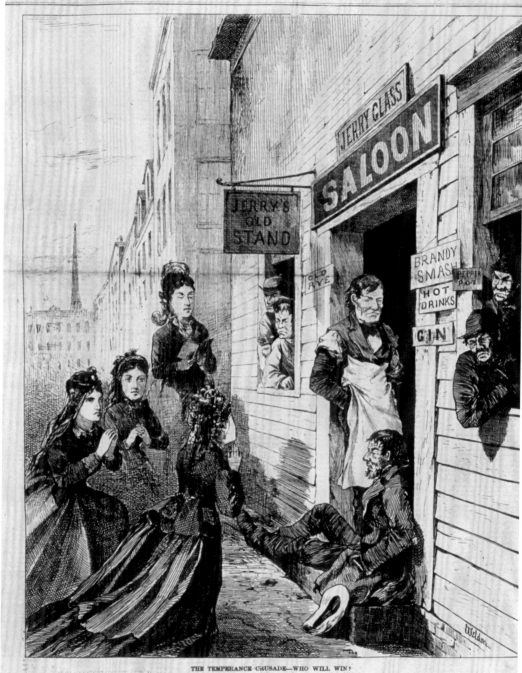

THE TEMPERANCE CRUSADE—WHO WILL WIN?

Women who supported temperance would go to taverns, singing hymns and praying to try and stop people from drinking.

The Women of Baraboo Wisconsin Launch Raids on Local Taverns

In the following excerpt from a 1927 article in the *Milwaukee Journal* newspaper, Mary A. Hartwell recalls a time more than seventy years earlier when she and other women of Baraboo, Wisconsin, launched raids on local taverns years before Carry Nation ever took a hatchet to saloons in Kansas. Hartwell says,

> It was in French Pete's place, a hotel on the hillside ... [where] the raid reached its climax. The Frenchman expected something and he was ready for us. As half the women approached the front of the hotel, Pete appeared at a window with a shotgun in his hand.
>
> "If any woman dares try to enter this place, I will shoot to kill," he threatened.
>
> And, at the same time, the other half of the women were at the back door, pouring Pete's liquor upon the ground so that it ran in rivulets down the street. Oh, that was great!
>
> There were some folks there, of course, that looked right sad as they saw the liquor going to waste, but most of 'em were in sympathy with the women. Husbands stood in the background and never raised a voice against what was being done. Lovers stood nearby, enjoying the bravery of their sweethearts.
>
> And there was one man, I remember, who remarked, "Well, mark my word, boys, the day will come when women will vote!"

Milwaukee Journal, "A Bottle Smashing Crusader of Wisconsin," *Milwaukee Journal*, 1927, www.wisconsinhistory.org/turningpoints/search.asp?id=1291.

"Mother Thompson and her Visitation Band" inspired other women across Ohio to form temperance groups of their own. Some of these groups also demanded that local saloonkeepers close their doors or risk seeing their stock of alcohol destroyed. Lewis, meanwhile, continued his public speeches. He also voiced support for the growing Women's Crusade. Convinced they were carrying out God's will, tens of thousands of women spread their crusade through the Midwestern states, West Virginia, New York, and as far west as Oregon and California.

Saloonkeepers React

These crusades, however, often provoked ridicule, anger, and violence from saloon owners and their customers. Threats, jeers, obscenities, and insults rained down upon the women as they protested. They were attacked, spit on, and soaked with dirty water and beer.

Some angry saloon proprietors set dogs loose on demonstrators. In Cincinnati, Ohio, an owner of a beer garden allegedly placed a cannon at the front door of his establishment and threatened to blow up anyone who dared to interfere with his business. Ruffians even dragged the seventy-year-old president of the Temperance League of Bucyrus, Ohio, through the streets.

According to Mattingly, newspapers of the day carried reports of women "drenched with paint; accosted with water from pumps and hoses; pelted with rotten eggs, stones, old boots, and even bricks; threatened by mobs so large and violent that police protection was inadequate; and forced by husbands to leave the streets. One spouse even publicly horsewhipped his wife for her participation."[32] Often police broke up these demonstrations and jailed the women, only to see them back on the streets after their release, once again agitating against alcohol.

Women's Crusade Dissolves

The Women's Crusade ran out of steam by the summer of 1874. Although it had attracted national attention, it had not done much to alter American drinking behaviors. The federal government had taken no action against drinking. Neither had state governments done much to promote temperance. In fact, saloons that had been closed by protestors reopened as the marches and demonstrations faded.

However, the Women's Crusade had not been a waste of time. For one thing, the women crusaders had helped to publicize temperance issues. Their

The women who stood up for temperance helped empower other women to find their voice in politics.

protests had revived other temperance groups. Their crusade had also encouraged many women from many social classes to organize and work with one another for a single purpose. Their protests did, at least temporarily, close thousands of bars and saloons across much of America.

By their example, the hymn-singing protestors also inspired other women to speak out against the serious social problem of drunkenness. By doing so, millions of women experienced for the first time a newfound feeling of purpose and accomplishment. They also tasted, at long last, the tang of political power.

Encouraged by these experiences, many women turned to other campaigns as well, such as the battle for women's suffrage—the right to vote. Temperance activist Amelia Bloomer wrote in her book, *The Lily*,

> We cannot consent to have woman remain silent on the Temperance question till she obtain her right of suffrage … we feel that day is too far distant for her to rest all her hopes and labors on that issue. Let her work with her whole heart in this cause and, while she demands a law that entirely prohibits the traffic in strong drink, let her also obtain a voice in making all laws by which she is to be governed.[33]

The work of the Women's Crusade also gave women a productive way to vent pent-up frustration against smothering traditions that had held them down for centuries. In fact, women's involvement in the fight against alcohol was far from over. This became apparent when many veterans of the Women's Crusade decided that their next step was to form a more disciplined, national organization. In November 1874, they met in Cleveland, Ohio, where they consolidated various state organizations to form the National Woman's Christian Temperance Union (WCTU).

Frances Willard Takes Charge

At the helm of the WCTU was a middle-aged woman named Frances Elizabeth Willard, a former educator, college administrator, daughter of pioneers, and an experienced temperance activist. Willard was also stern, intelligent, wry, powerful, and capable of leading a national organization. An accomplished writer, public speaker, and advocate of women's rights, she was attracted to the temperance movement because she admired the way women had taken over a crusade left unfinished by men. She also was an ardent opponent of saloons, convinced that they contributed to the dominance of men over women and excluded women from public life.

From the start, controversy divided the membership of the WCTU over the main purpose of the organization. One faction, made up of conservative wealthy women, wanted the WCTU to focus solely on temperance issues. Willard and her supporters, however, argued that the organization should adopt a more wide-ranging approach that also zeroed in on an array of social and economic problems

The National Woman's Christian Temperance Union (WCTU) became a powerful advocate to many progressive causes.

bedeviling American society. Willard insisted that problems such as poverty, bad health, and squalid living conditions led to the curse of drunkenness that resulted in the abuse of women and children.

Willard soon emerged the victor in the dispute and took control of the WCTU. Under her leadership, the organization became a powerful advocate of many progressive causes. In addition to its battle against alcohol abuse, the WCTU encouraged women from all walks of life to learn more about nutritional cooking, gardening, health, and exercise. It supported, among other things, not only the women's suffrage movement, but also civil service reform, assistance to Native Americans, and the rights of workers to organize unions to improve their pay

and working conditions. Also on its agenda were plans to ban drugs and improve personal morals.

Willard believed that something more than hard work and dedication was propelling the WCTU and other progressives toward reform. There was also, she thought, divine guidance. "These organized movements," she suggested, "are, as we think, God's great recruiting station for the new war in which He is enrolling, drilling and disciplining."[34]

As chief spokesperson for the WCTU, Willard agreed with social critics who believed that alcohol caused people to be poor; however, she also pointed out that it was equally true that men drank liquor to escape poverty and squalid living

Frances Willard's Work Day

Educator, suffragist, and author Frances Willard also worked tirelessly as the president of the Woman's Christian Temperance Union. Her last interview before her death was with *Our Day* magazine and it provides a glimpse of her busy schedule:

> The earliest book in the day, before breakfast, if possible, is a book of devotion: either the New Testament or a volume of texts and comments like "Daily Strength for Daily Needs." After breakfast I glance over the daily papers. Then, at perhaps 9 o'clock, I call my stenographer and dictate articles and letters continuously for eight hours, with an intercession of half an hour for luncheon.... Today, a memorial must be written to the authorities of every college in the United States, showing with tact and an attempt at least at sweet reasonableness why the territory adjacent to a college ought to be under prohibition. Tomorrow, a memorial to the authorities of the National Library at Washington, showing why intoxicating liquors as a beverage should not be sold in the library restaurant. The next day a form of statute must be carefully prepared, in consultation with the best legal minds, and sent out to the state W. C. T. U. presidents, urging that it be taken as a basis for the winter's legislative work.
>
> Editorials and other articles must be written for the press.... Sketches of workers of which there are thousands, must be written up in sympathetic and intelligent characterization. Letters must be read and replied to by thousand upon thousand.

Quoted in George T.B. Davis, "The Greatest American Woman," *Our Day*, vol. 18, March 1898, http:// prohibition.osu.edu/willard/willard_last_interview.cfm.

conditions. Thus, she argued, it was important to improve the social conditions that drove people to drink.

Above all, however, the WCTU never lost sight of its main mission: to abolish liquor on the state and local levels. Many of its members also called for a constitutional amendment to prohibit liquor nationwide. To accomplish these goals, Willard launched a national campaign to build popular support. Across America the WCTU produced and distributed vast quantities of books, pamphlets, newspapers, magazines, and other documents calling for a ban on alcohol. WCTU speakers took every opportunity to convince audiences about the evils of Demon Rum. Women volunteers across the country also circulated petitions, formed pressure groups, and lobbied lawmakers to rid America of alcohol abuse.

Celebrating Going Dry

Even before Prohibition, many towns and counties across the United States voted to become "dry." In the following excerpt a woman known only as Mrs. Stuckenberger addresses an audience of young people in Cambridge, Massachusetts, during the town's tenth annual celebration of being alcohol-free. Mrs. Stuckenberger says,

> I congratulate you children that you do not know what it is to see a saloon in your city.... When I was a little girl ... my schoolhouse was surrounded by saloons.... I used to hear the screaming of the children because a drunken father was whipping them ... we ... were often frightened by the sight of bloody, fighting men ... not only the common ignorant people but [also] ... men who were called gentlemen.... On one side of my father's grounds lived a brewer. He had two sons, nice, bright boys, but the oldest died young ... of drinking.... The other lives yet ... ruined because he cannot keep sober.... On the other side was a doctor. His oldest son was a man to be proud of, but his father began to keep a drugstore, where he sold drinks of liquor, and this promising son ... died of drunkenness after making wife and children very unhappy and also very poor.

Quoted in J.C. Furnas, *The Americans: A Social History of the United States 1587–1914*, New York: Putnam's, 1969, pp. 136–37.

The Fading Influence of the WCTU

Convinced that drinking alcohol was deeply etched into American society, the WCTU leadership decided to take its organization's message directly to America's youth. In 1886 the group had persuaded New York lawmakers to make antidrinking education mandatory in state public schools. By the end of the century, most other states had done the same. During this period, the U.S. Congress also mandated that WCTU's educational programs become part of the curriculum for schools under federal control in Washington, D.C., and in U.S. territories, such as Puerto Rico and Guam.

WCTU's books and pamphlets instructed millions of American students in the late nineteenth century about the dangers of alcohol. Among other things, young children were taught that alcohol was a colorless, liquid poison that harmed human health and led to insanity.

In addition to promoting education, the WCTU became politically active. For example, it supported the Prohibition Party, a national political party begun in 1869. WCTU leaders took this action because by now they were convinced that

The WCTU leaders supported the Prohibition Party, thinking a national party could pass prohibition laws more effectively.

the only way to close the loopholes found in so many state prohibition laws was to support a national political party that called for federal prohibition of the manufacture, sale, and transportation of liquor. At the time, no other major political party favored such a radical solution.

Then without much warning, the WCTU lost its powerful leader when Willard died in 1898 at the age of fifty-nine, possibly of influenza. She was mourned and praised by Americans everywhere. Tributes to her came from an array of public speakers across America. Black flags appeared at half-staff in New York, Chicago, and Washington, D.C., announcing her passing. Schools were named in her honor, and her birthday became a holiday in many states.

Willard also became the first woman to be represented in Statuary Hall in the U.S. Capitol in Washington, D.C.

Her death severely and permanently weakened the organization she had led to national prominence. Not only had Willard been a vigorous and steady leader, but she was also personally associated with the identity of the organization. Her personality had been the driving force of the WCTU and now it was gone. Although the WCTU carried on without her, it ceased to be the same powerful social, moral, and political force in America. Another antialcohol movement was underway, however, that would eventually eclipse the WCTU and pave the way for a national ban on alcohol.

Chapter Four

The Anti-Saloon Campaign Takes Charge

America's saloons became the primary target for temperance workers and prohibitionists in the 1890s. These drinking places were common features of everyday life. One estimate holds that there was a licensed saloon for every three hundred people of the nation. And in 1909 there may have been as many as fifty thousand illegal, unlicensed saloons. Some of them were well managed and richly decorated with polished wood, brass trim, chandeliers, and marble statuary, often catering to wealthy patrons in big cities. Many other saloons, however, were unclean, run-down, urine-soaked buildings with swinging doors and spittoons that were frequented by drunkards, gamblers, and prostitutes. "The most notable thing about the saloon was its stink," writes Donald Barr Chidsey. "It was a fusty, musty odor, damp and clammy, an odor compounded of sawdust, tobacco juice, malt, metal polish, and whiskey."[35]

Here many intoxicated men ruined their health, squandered their family's savings, and staggered home in a drunken haze to abuse their wives and children. A growing number of Americans watched these daily dramas in their own neighborhoods with disgust and alarm. Now and then local governments took action against saloons for the safety of the public. Such was the case on March 9, 1896, when the City Council of Lansing, Michigan, under pressure from local citizens, took back the liquor license of the Oklahoma Saloon, because the saloon was considered "a rendezvous for characters which make the place a menace to God, order, and the safety of our citizens."[36]

Nonetheless, saloons remained popular gathering places for many of America's drinkers of alcohol. They also became places that many antialcohol activists hated passionately.

Billy Sunday

One of America's most-beloved and outspoken foes of saloons was the flamboyant Billy Sunday. Born into poverty in Iowa, Sunday played professional baseball as a young man for the Chicago White Stockings, earning a reputation for speed in stealing bases on the field.

Evangelist Billy Sunday was energetically outspoken about the sins of drinking.

A frequenter of saloons, he gave up alcohol after embracing Evangelical Christianity one Sunday in 1887 after listening to the songs and testimonials of a band of workers at the Pacific Garden Rescue Mission in Chicago. Within a few years, Sunday gave up a promising baseball career to become a traveling evangelical preacher in the Midwest, who zealously campaigned against alcohol and especially saloons.

Employing a mix of showmanship, physical antics, and verbal skills tinged with humor, Sunday spread his conservative Christian views on alcohol abuse, singling out the saloon as a great evil while making lots of money in the process. "The saloon is a coward," he thundered in one of his sermons. "It is a thief … [that] robs you of manhood and leaves you in rags and takes away your friends, and it robs your family. It impoverishes your children and it brings insanity and suicide."[37]

As his popularity increased, so did his staff, which at times numbered as many as fifty, including musicians, singers, secretaries, and carpenters who erected a makeshift tabernacle each time he arrived in a new town. Scandal-free, wholesome, and sincere, Sunday became one of America's favorite preachers.

Many historians agree that his antialcohol ministry—which as many as a million people may have attended in American big cities during the early 1900s—did much to help pave the way for the Eighteenth Amendment to the U.S. Constitution, which banned alcohol across the United States. Sunday seemed to think

the nation was heading toward that same goal. "I tell you that the curse of God Almighty is on the saloon," Sunday insisted. "Legislatures are legislating against it. Decent society is barring it out."[38]

The Hatchetations of Carry Nation

While Billy Sunday was adored by millions of Americans, the public was less sure what to make of the most notorious enemy of the nation's saloons—a controversial woman, who was willing to use violence against drinking establishments in the name of God. Born Carry Amelia Moore, this aggressive reformer spent her

Carry Nation wielded a hatchet and was willing to use violence against drinking establishments.

childhood in Garrard County, Kentucky, where she endured the antics of her delusional mother, who believed she was Queen Victoria of England. Carry was also greatly troubled during her youth from watching her grandfather overindulge in alcohol every morning at breakfast.

Her dislike of alcohol developed into hatred years later when she suffered from a brief and unhappy marriage to an alcoholic in 1867 who died six months after the marriage ceremony. Adding to her lasting sorrow was a daughter named Charlien, who grew up to be a mentally troubled adult who habitually drank liquor. Although Carry loved and cared for Charlien as much as she could, she harbored a lingering anger for her departed husband, whom Carry believed, had somehow passed on his addiction to their offspring.

Carry remarried in 1874. This time her husband, nineteen years her senior, was David Nation, a wandering preacher whose black clothes and flowing white beard reminded people of an Old Testament preacher. After moving around the South for several years, the family, which included David's children from a previous marriage, settled in Medicine Lodge, Kansas, in 1889. It was here that Nation, now in her fifties, helped to found a chapter of the National Woman's Christian Temperance Union (WCTU).

Infuriated that saloons in the state openly sold alcohol in defiance of Kansas' unenforced prohibition laws, Nation employed the tactics of other WCTU members by singing and praying outside the saloons and taverns, hoping to convince the owners to close them. Fearless and bold, she also confronted patrons as they entered the drinking establishments and called them names and implored them to give up drinking.

Her work did little to stop alcohol sales. Her methods, however, radically changed one spring day in 1900 when she became convinced that she had received a revelation from God who commanded her to take decisive action against drinking. Nation later recalled,

> I was awakened by a voice which seemed to me speaking in my heart, these words, "GO TO KIOWA," and my hands were lifted and thrown down and the words, "I'LL STAND BY YOU." The words, "Go to Kiowa," were spoken in a murmuring, musical tone, low and soft, but "I'll stand by you," was very clear, positive and emphatic. I was impressed with a great inspiration, the interpretation was very plain, and it was this: "Take something in your hands, and throw at these places in Kiowa and smash them." I was very much relieved and overjoyed and was determined to be, "obedient to the heavenly vision."[39]

After this episode, an inspired Nation soon barged into the saloons of the sleepy, small town of Kiowa and threw bricks, rocks, scrap metal, and pieces of wood, breaking liquor bottles and inflicting property damage. She also wielded a hatchet—which became her trademark—to destroy bottles of spirits and bar room property. By 1900 Nation was an imposing figure who no one could intimidate. Standing 6 feet (1.8m) tall, weighing 180 pounds, and often dressed in black, she described herself as "a bull-dog running along at the feet of Jesus, barking at what he doesn't like."[40]

When local authorities threatened to jail her for destruction of private property, she promptly pointed out that she had merely destroyed alcoholic beverages that were forbidden by law. She walked away free. Carry Nation, however, was not yet finished in her battle against liquor. Next, she and other like-minded women attacked saloons in Wichita, Kansas, and elsewhere, where they destroyed bottles and kegs of liquor, as well as plate-glass windows, paintings, and other property. "I came to the Governor's town to destroy the finest saloon in it," she said, "hoping thus to attract public attention to the flagrant

Carry Nation Makes the News

Carry Nation drew media attention when she attacked the property of saloonkeepers in her crusade against alcohol. This edited account from an anonymous writer in the *Topeka Daily Capital* newspaper tells what happened when Nation arrived in Wichita, Kansas, on December 27, 1900:

Mrs. Carry Nation, president of Barber County Women's Christian Temperance Union, began today a raid on the saloons in Wichita. As a result of her work she is now under arrest and placed behind the bars at the county jail.

At 9:45 this morning she entered the saloon in the basement of the Carey hotel and without a word of warning pulled from a bundle of papers which she carried in her hands two large stones. Before the clerks and bartenders could realize what was going on, Mrs. Nation sent one of the stones whizzing through large oil painting of Cleopatra nude at the Roman bath. The painting was valued at $100. As a result of the stone hitting the painting the picture is completely spoiled.

After damaging this picture, the woman suddenly turned herself about and … sent another large stone through a valuable $1,500 mirror which is situated directly back of the bar. She then left the saloon.

While in the saloon she also broke about $25 worth of bottled goods and also a window. As soon as she left the saloon she was arrested.

Quoted in David Colbert, ed., *Eyewitness to America: 500 Years of America in the Words of Those Who Saw It Happen*, New York: Pantheon, 1997, pp. 309–10.

violation of a Kansas law, under the very eye of the chief executive of the state."[41]

Authorities arrested her more than thirty times during her spree of attacks that lasted until March 12, 1901. At this point, she announced on the pages of her publication, *The Smasher's Mail*, that although she would give up violent acts, she would continue her war against alcohol.

In addition to waging violence against saloons, Nation often engaged in other questionable acts. For example, in a 1901 open letter to children, placed in the *Topeka Daily Capital* newspaper, Nation wrote,

> I send you greetings and ask you to help me destroy that which is on the streets and protected by the police and the city officials to destroy you, my darlings. I want every one of you little ones to grab up a rock and smash the glass doors and windows of these hell-holes. You will do your duty and enroll your name of the pages of undying fame, and place yourself on the side of God and humanity.[42]

There were other extremist remarks. For instance, she celebrated the assassination of President William McKinley, killed by an anarchist in 1901, because, she said, he drank alcohol and got what he deserved.

Although Nation generated publicity for herself and the issue of temperance, the WCTU eventually decided that her antics did more harm than good and tried to keep the organization from being identified with her. Eventually, despite her good intentions, she became a figure of public ridicule. Her marriage dissolved and her husband divorced her. "My life has been made miserable by this woman,"[43] he once complained. She died in obscurity on June 9, 1911, and was buried in an unmarked grave in Belton, Missouri.

Pussyfoot Johnson

Carry Nation was not the only prohibitionist to be aggressive with saloons. Another colorful figure, often called the "Male Carry Nation," was also smashing illegal saloons and containers of alcohol. He also carried weapons. But unlike Carry Nation, William Johnson fought and arrested lawbreakers.

As a young man, Johnson earned his living as a journalist and teacher in Coventry, New York. He later moved to Nebraska, where he worked as a cowboy. Here, in 1881, Johnson's lifelong opposition to alcohol led him to work with state antialcohol forces hoping to make prohibition part of the state constitution. In this struggle, Johnson showed his willingness to even use deceptive measures for a cause in which he believed. Once, posing as a brewery owner, he corresponded with alcohol industry officials to gain useful information about their tactics in fighting prohibitionists, which he published for the nation to read.

In 1906 Johnson was working as a lobbyist for the prohibition movement in Washington, D.C., when President Teddy Roosevelt sent him to the Indian/Oklahoma Territory to lead an effort to stop the illegal liquor trade that was devastating Native Americans. At the time, this region was still a wild and lawless land where men settled grudges with guns.

Pussyfoot Johnson smashed beer kegs and whiskey bottles and closed many saloons.

Johnson and his men raided illegal local liquor dealers. Because of his quiet, catlike manner of sneaking up on his prey, Johnson quickly earned the nickname "Pussyfoot." However, there was nothing secretive about the way Johnson—who wore a cowboy hat and a long coat and carried a rifle—would smash whisky bottles and beer kegs, as he and his men closed down thousands of illegal bars and arrested thousands of lawbreakers, including those who smuggled liquor into Indian territory.

During his stint as a federal lawman, Johnson took part in a dozen fistfights. There were shoot-outs too, during which some of his men were killed. Johnson also endured many death threats. Once, upon learning that a saloonkeeper had sworn to kill him, an infuriated Johnson disguised himself, rode into town on a horse, sauntered into the bar and arrested him. By the time Pussyfoot Johnson left the Indian territory in 1911, he and his

agents had made six thousand arrests and closed down many saloons. He returned east and took over a publishing plant that was pouring out propaganda for a growing organization that would rival and then eclipse the WCTU. It would also prove powerful enough to pave the way for national prohibition.

The Rise of the Anti-Saloon League

The new powerhouse was the Anti-Saloon League (ASL), founded in 1893 by Howard Russell, a Protestant minister in Ohio. Like many other temperance groups, the league wanted to close down the state's saloons—places many Ohioans viewed as violent breeding grounds of drunkenness that ruined families, led girls into prostitution, and encouraged working men to squander their wages on alcohol instead of taking care of their loved ones. Although closing saloons topped its agenda, the league also had a bigger prize in mind; it wanted new laws that banned alcohol nationwide. Much of the organization's strength lay in how it was structured. Its membership was a vast confederation of churches, including evangelicals, Methodists, Baptists, members of the Church of Christ, and other denominations. The Anti-Saloon League viewed these churches as both vehicles for carrying out temperance work and sources of revenue.

Russell asked a brilliant Ohio attorney, Wayne B. Wheeler, to take charge of the organization in 1901. Convinced that America was in a period of moral decline, Wheeler accepted the offer and soon proved himself to be a stern, tough, honest commander of a huge, potent organization. He also became a shrewd and powerful political figure in both Ohio and national politics. During his heyday, he could be counted on to influence

An Alabama Representative Calls for National Prohibition

Alabama congressman Richmond P. Hobson spoke on the floor of the House of Representatives on December 22, 1914, in support of a proposed prohibition amendment. In his speech he said,

[The purpose] … of this resolution … is to destroy the agency that debauches [corrupts] the youth of the land and thereby perpetuates [achieves] its hold upon the Nation. The resolution … does not coerce [pressure] any drinker. It simply says that barter and sale … shall not continue the debauching of the youth. Now, the Liquor Trust [industry] are wise enough to know that they can not perpetuate their sway [influence] by depending on debauching grown people, so they [try to teach] … the young to drink. Now we apply exactly the same method to destroy them. We do not try to force old drinkers to stop drinking, but we do effectively put an end to the systematic, organized debauching of our youth through thousands and tens of thousands of agencies throughout the land. Men here may try to escape the simplicity of this problem. They can not. Some are trying to defend alcohol by saying that its abuse only is bad and that its temperate use is all right. Science absolutely denies it, and proclaims that drunkenness does not produce one-tenth part of the harm to society that the widespread, temperate, moderate drinking does. Some say it is adulteration that harms. Some are trying to say that it is only distilled liquors that do harm. Science comes in now and says that all alcohol does harm.

Quoted in K. Austin Kerr, *The Politics of Moral Behavior: Prohibition and Drug Abuse*, Reading, MA: Addison-Wesley, 1973, http://prohibition.osu.edu/content/hobson.cfm.

enough voters to oust any elected officials who opposed the league.

As was the case for so many temperance leaders, Wheeler had a relative who had been ravaged by alcohol. In addition, a drunken farmhand had accidentally wounded Wheeler with a pitchfork when Wheeler was a youth. These bitter memories spurred him to fight for national prohibition.

In 1917 Wheeler served as the Anti-Saloon League's chief attorney; two years later he led the organization to national prominence. He did this by adopting a strategy of helping prohibition candidates to win at city and county levels. These local political bases could then be used to launch bigger campaigns in state and federal elections. The league also favored no political party; instead it backed any candidate that voiced promises to back prohibition laws. If all candidates were proalcohol or "wets," as people were calling them, the league ran its own "dry" candidates for public office. Wheeler's long-term goal was to rid America of alcohol. First, however, the league fought to close the saloons.

Targeting Saloons Sets off New Controversies

By the late nineteenth century, the anti-alcohol forces had new reasons for opposing saloons. At the time America was experiencing a great wave of immigration. The newcomers came largely from Southern and Eastern Europe. Most were illiterate, poor, and did not speak English. They also tended to be Catholics, Orthodox Christians, or Jews from countries such as Italy, Greece, Poland, Romania, and Russia, which made them different from America's rural populations that were mostly Protestants and descendants of Anglo-Saxon stock of Northern Europe. Newly arrived Germans, who congregated in American big cities, tended to support moderate drinking. In addition, millions of Irish people who had a long tradition of drinking liquor, poured into the nation's urban areas.

Many of America's newest arrivals lacked work skills, education, and experience and were therefore forced to accept low-paying, hard jobs in dangerous factories and slaughterhouses in the big cities. They lived in overcrowded and unsanitary apartments. When they were not working, they often sought refuge and friendship from their hard lives in neighborhood saloons. Here they met with friends, relatives, fellow workers, and union members to socialize, relax, and have fun.

Nonetheless, many traditional, native-born Americans, meanwhile, were unsympathetic to the new immigrants and their desire to frequent saloons. They feared losing their own jobs, culture, language, and customs to the newly arrived strangers who congregated to drink in the ill-regarded saloons. Their fear motivated hundreds of thousands of Americans to support the Anti-Saloon League.

Battle lines were forming over the issue of prohibition. Increasingly, the prohibition forces found strength in the rural areas of the country. Arrayed against them were big city political machines, and the foreign born. Religious affiliation also played a role. Protestant Christians tended to be "dry" and Catholics "wet" on the issue of prohibition.

League Victories

By 1905 state prohibition was still in effect only in Kansas, Maine, and North Dakota. But the Anti-Saloon League and its allies revived state prohibition. Within four years West Virginia, Tennessee, North Carolina, Georgia, Oklahoma, and Mississippi also joined the movement with new state prohibition laws. These gains, however, took place in agricultural states in the South and the Midwest, where most residents led rural, religious, and conservative lives. The industrial, urban states remained wet.

In fact, millions of Americans continued to drink heavily, even in the dry states. Again drinkers of hard drink discovered loopholes in their state prohibition laws that allowed them to purchase liquor through the mail. Trainloads filled with crates of bottled liquor rattled into dry states from neighboring wet states every day, making a mockery of the new dry laws.

The Anti-Saloon League, however, responded by persuading U.S. senator William S. Kenyon of Iowa and North Carolina representative Edwin Y. Webb to draft legislation that enabled state governments, instead of the federal government, to regulate train shipments of liquor across state borders. Congress approved the bill, but President William Howard Taft vetoed it, claiming the legislation violated the U.S. Constitution by

Millions of Americans continued to drink heavily, even in the dry states.

curbing the federal government's right to regulate commerce.

Congress, however, overrode Taft's veto with the necessary two-thirds majority vote. The U.S. Supreme Court later ruled in *Clark Distillery Co. v. Western Maryland Railroad Co.* that the law was constitutional. Such a powerful show of support at the national level shocked the wets. It clearly demonstrated that the drys were no longer merely a regional political force in the farming states. In fact, some political observers at the time were so impressed with the league's demonstration of power that they predicted prohibition at the national level was only a matter of time.

Chapter Five

Setting the Stage for National Prohibition

The Anti-Saloon League pushed harder. During a blizzard in Columbus, Ohio, in November 1913, at a national convention, league members noisily approved a resolution that called for national prohibition. A month later five thousand people from across the nation arrived in Washington, D.C., to attend a public demonstration organized by the Anti-Saloon League and the National Woman's Christian Temperance Union (WCTU). They marched in the cold and snow along Pennsylvania Avenue from the White House to the Capitol, and they demanded that Congress amend the U.S. Constitution with the Eighteenth Amendment to prohibit the sale and manufacture of alcohol in the entire country. Later that same day, sympathetic lawmakers presented bills to Congress and the U.S. Senate, written by the Anti-Saloon League, calling for the amendment process to begin.

Wayne B. Wheeler and the league, however, did not rush Congress to vote on the issue just yet. They wanted time to build strong political support for national prohibition among voters across the country. They also wanted to back dry candidates running for Congress in the upcoming 1914 nationwide election.

A powerful political campaign soon got underway. For the next year, the league printed and distributed tons of letters and brochures and sent telegrams and letters to elected officials across the country. Workers circulated petitions and made speeches in support of prohibition candidates.

Meanwhile, companies and businesses with the most to lose if prohibition became law—namely the manufacturers, distributors, and retail sellers of liquor, beer, and wine—took part in the growing national debate. They struck back with angry words and political lobbying, but they were no match for the impassioned,

Industrialist Henry Ford claimed that hungover and drunk workers on his assembly line were unproductive and dangerous.

well-organized, and well-financed temperance forces.

Other business leaders supported prohibition. Among them were industrialists, such as Henry Ford and Henry Clay Frick, who urged cracking down on drinking. Drunken workers or workers with hangovers, they argued, were unproductive and dangerous, especially around machinery in factories.

Many labor organizations agreed. During negotiations with factory owners in recent years, some union negotiators promised factory owners sober workers in exchange for safer working conditions, higher wages, an eight-hour work day, and other benefits. The Knights of the Brotherhood of Locomotive Engineers and various railroad unions were among the labor organizations that promoted various temperance measures.

The Progressive Movement Supports Prohibition

The prohibition movement had still other sources of support. By this time, antiliquor efforts had become part of a larger reform movement underway across the country. Called the progressive movement, this national crusade focused on a wide range of social, economic, and political problems that had developed in the young industrializing nation. Crusading journalists, small businessmen and women, educators, reform-minded politicians, and many others had joined forces to make the new

Billy Sunday Decries Alcoholic Idiots

Billy Sunday, professional baseball player turned evangelical temperance preacher, denounced alcohol to millions of Americans. In one of his speeches to a Boston, Massachusetts, audience, he said,

> Listen! Seventy-five per cent of our idiots come from intemperate parents, 80 per cent of the paupers, 82 per cent of the crime is committed by men under the influence of liquor, 90 per cent of the adult criminals are whiskey made. The *Chicago Tribune* kept track for 10-years and found that 53,438 murders were committed in the saloons.... I step up to a young man on the scaffold and say, "what brought you here?" Drink! Whence all the misery and sorrow and corruption? Invariably it is drink.
>
> Whiskey and beer are all right in their place, but their place is in hell. The saloon hasn't one leg to stand on ... Five Points, in New York, was a spot as near like hell as any spot on earth. There are five streets that run to this point, and right in the middle was an old brewery, and the streets on either side were lined with grog shops.... Look at Kansas. It is dry. In 85 of 105 counties in Kansas there is not one idiot. In 38 counties they have not a single pauper in the poorhouse, and there are only 600 dependents in the whole State. In 65 counties in Kansas they did not have a single prisoner in the county jails in the year 1912, and in some of the counties the grand jury hasn't been called to try a criminal case in 10 years.

Billy Sunday, "Booze," sermon given in Boston, Massachusetts, Billy Sunday Online, http://billysunday .org/sermons/booze.html.

nation a less-corrupt, fairer, and more decent place in which to live. Meanwhile, the ongoing suffrage movement, which was also gaining momentum, continued to highlight the concerns of women damaged by alcohol abuse.

Another blow to alcohol interests came in 1913 when the passage of the Sixteenth Amendment to the U.S. Constitution authorized Congress to levy taxes on personal incomes, thus making it harder for wets to argue that Americans needed to keep alcohol legal to raise revenue for the government. In that same year, Americans saw their nation adopt another constitutional change—the Seventeenth Amendment—that allowed them to directly elect their U.S. senators. This expansion in democracy gave drys increased opportunities to influence lawmakers.

Singing Against Saloons

Members of the Woman's Christian Temperance Union (WCTU) used a variety of means to fight alcohol, including singing songs outside saloons. The following song, set to the tune of "Yankee Doodle," is one of the songs they sang.

Saloons have been by Lincoln tried …
And drinking has been easy.
And many of our men and boys
Occasionally are boozy.

Chorus

Lincoln now is going dry
Yankee doodle dandy,
Saloons have met their "Waterloo"
Strong drink no more is handy.

We will no longer give consent
Our sons are far too precious,
We now unite saloons to rout
And ask the Lord to help us.

Chorus

Let all now join the Civic League
And help to clean up Lincoln
And if we turn these leeches out
Some poor folks will have plenty.

Chorus

Our buildings would soon fill again
And business go a humming,
When people spend their money right
And quit their foolish bumming.

Chorus

Quoted in Nebraska Woman's Christian Temperance Union, *Nebraska's Favorite Temperance Rallying Songs*, Nebraska Woman's Christian Temperance Union, 1908, www.nebraskastudies.org/0700/frameset_reset. html?http://www.nebraskastudies.org/0700/stories/0701_0122.html.

Nearing Victory

In 1914 several new dry representatives took seats in Congress. However, prohibition proponents were still not sure whether they had the support of two-thirds of the lawmakers needed to start the process for changing the U.S. Constitution with an amendment.

Nonetheless, dry legislators introduced a resolution on December 22 calling for a debate on the issue. For the moment, they only wanted to know where other lawmakers stood on the issue. At last, the House voted and revealed that 197 legislators favored prohibition, and 190 were against it.

The prohibition movement soon received another boost with the outbreak of World War I in the summer of 1914. Once again armed conflict played a decisive role in the fate of alcohol in America.

World War I: A Turning Point

By the second decade of the twentieth century, Europe was headed for war. Decades of suspicion, political intrigue, nationalism, militarism, empire building, ethnic rivalries, and territorial disputes had set the stage for international calamity. By 1914 two hostile camps faced one another: the Triple Entente (France, Russia, and Great Britain) and the Triple Alliance (Germany, Austria-Hungary, and Italy). Europe was a powder keg waiting to explode. The spark came with the assassination of the heir to the throne of the Austrian-Hungary Empire at the hands of Serbian terrorists on June 28, 1914.

During the coming months, European nations, honoring their commitments to support their allies, declared war upon one another. When European empires brought their colonies into the fray, the war became global.

At first, the United States managed to remain neutral. However, public sentiment tilted toward Great Britain, thanks to a common language, similar culture, and shared support for a democratic government.

America Joins the War

As the war progressed, America became increasingly anti-German. Many Americans were leery of a country with a dictatorship controlled by an emperor and the military. They were also upset that Germany had invaded Belgium, a nation whose neutrality had been guaranteed by a treaty. Germany also alienated Americans when it secretly schemed—unsuccessfully—to convince Mexico to join the war against the United States. Finally, Americans became enraged over Germany's use of unrestricted submarine warfare that resulted in the sinking of U.S. vessels.

At last the United States declared war on Germany on April 12, 1917. Smoldering anger against Germany now turned to hysteria, as nationalist Americans looked for scapegoats at home. Many German Americans lost their jobs. Some were attacked and accused of disloyalty to the United States. German literature, music, and language courses were plucked from school curriculums. Zealots insisted on renaming popular German food; sauerkraut became "liberty cabbage," and bratwurst was changed to "hot dog."

Beer Becomes Unpatriotic

Meanwhile, prohibitionists acted quickly to use the wartime hysteria for their own purpose. Criticism rained down on the beer industry. Extremists proclaimed that German American brewers were traitors and spies. They also questioned the loyalty of German Americans who belonged to various German ethnic political and civic organizations. Moreover, many prohibitionists argued, Americans should stop drinking beer because it was the drink of the enemy. They insisted that money not spent on beer could be better used for more patriotic causes.

Under pressure from the Anti-Saloon League, dry congressmen pushed legislation that ensured that all grains and other foodstuffs were used to feed American soldiers, sailors, and allies and not as mash for distilled liquor. Dry lawmakers argued that because children were starving in war-torn Europe, it was wrong to divert enough grain to bake 11 million of loaves of bread a day to the liquor industry to make alcoholic drinks instead.

Next antiprohibition lawmakers inserted provisions in a proposed food bill which, if passed by Congress, would ban the use of grain to make liquor. The prospect of such a law worried President Woodrow Wilson. Although he wanted to make sure sufficient grain supplies were delivered to U.S. military personnel, he

German soldiers shown drinking beer while burning a city. Americans viewed beer as unpatriotic during the World Wars because of its connection with Germany.

also opposed any law that also would cut off federal taxes from the alcohol industry in time of war. Seeking a compromise, he persuaded dry legislators to withdraw the controversial provisions of the food bill and promised that prohibition would be part of future legislation. But in September 1918, leading dry congressmen were convinced that Wilson had not acted quickly enough on his promise and voted to ban the use of grain for any beverage. The president, now believing that the Congress would override a veto, chose not to oppose the bill and signed it.

Congress Debates the Eighteenth Amendment

In 1917 the drys forced Congress to take up an even stronger prohibition measure: the proposed Eighteenth Amendment to

The U.S. Government Studies the Effectiveness of Prohibition

In 1926 a U.S. Senate subcommittee held hearings to investigate the effects of Prohibition. Speaking in favor of keeping restrictions on alcohol was Ella A. Boole, president of the Woman's Christian Temperance Movement from 1925 to 1933. Boole said,

The closing of the open saloon with its doors swinging both ways, an ever-present invitation for all to drink—men, women, and boys—is an outstanding fact, and no one wants it to return. It has resulted in better national health, children are born under better conditions, homes are better, and the mother is delivered from the fear of a drunken husband. There is better food. Savings-banks deposits have increased, and many a man has a bank account to-day who had none in the days of the saloon.

The increase in home owning is another evidence that money wasted in drink is now used for the benefit of the family. Improved living conditions are noticeable in our former slum districts....

Safety-first campaigns on railroad in the presence of the increasing number of automobiles are greatly strengthened by prohibition....

Life-insurance companies have long known that drinkers were poor risks, but they recognize the fact that prohibition has removed a preventable cause of great financial loss to them....

Your attention has been called to the failures [of Prohibition]. We claim these have been the result of lax enforcement. The machinery of enforcement should be strengthened.

Quoted in Margaret C. Moran, ed., *U.S. History and Government, Readings and Documents*, New York: AMSCO School Publications, 2003, p. 181.

the U.S. Constitution. During heated arguments over the issue, antiprohibitionists in the Senate made a big mistake. Confident that the amendment did not have support from at least thirty-six states needed to ratify it—even though by now twenty-seven states had state prohibition laws of some sort—they agreed to let the amendment go forward, provided that ratification by the states was completed within six years.

Consideration of the Eighteenth Amendment

After the Senate approved the bill, the House of Representatives took up the issue and quickly approved the Eighteenth Amendment on December 18, 1917, which clearly prohibited "the manufacture, sale, or transportation of intoxicating liquors." The bill also extended the time limit for state approval of the measure to seven years. Next the measure went to the states for ratification.

And as the states pondered the amendment proposal, congressional drys pushed through an emergency law—despite earlier assurances they would not do so—that imposed wartime prohibition on the nation. This legal action, however, did not become effective until November 21, 1918, just ten days before World War I came to an end. Nonetheless, the new law proved useful to the foes of alcohol, who now argued that a postwar America

should be alcohol-free. And what better way to do this, they maintained, than by linking wartime prohibition with the current national effort to change the Constitution to banish liquor forever?

One state after another quickly ratified the amendment. Contrary to what many wet lawmakers had expected, there was huge support for prohibition in the country. Decades of propaganda and lobbying by the Anti-Saloon League, other temperance groups, and churches had convinced millions of Americans that the nation should abolish alcohol from the marketplace. By January 16, 1919—a little more than a year after World War I ended—the Nebraska state

Political cartoon showing both political parties avoiding the prohibition issue after it went into effect.

legislature ratified the Eighteenth Amendment. Three-fourths of the states had now said yes to the amendment. National prohibition had arrived.

Addressing a Flawed Amendment

Dry and wets alike were astonished by how fast prohibition had come upon them. They also realized that the newest amendment to the U.S. Constitution had flaws that had been overlooked as it was rushed through Congress. The amendment, for example, banned the manufacture, sale, transport, import, and export of alcoholic beverages, but said nothing about curbing the buying and drinking of liquor. Thus, Americans could still legally obtain alcohol—even if produced illegally—and store it in their homes. Nor did the new amendment explain how prohibition would be enforced against those who did produce and sell liquor and fermented drinks. Would enforcement be a federal responsibility, or that of the states? Critics also pointed out that the Constitution guarantees all Americans the right to be secure in their homes. They warned that this right could be abused if overzealous law enforcement personnel felt compelled to raid private homes looking for alcohol.

Wayne B. Wheeler, working with House Judiciary Committee chairman Andrew J. Volstead

of Minnesota and other lawmakers, tackled this issue by writing new legislation that sought a balance between enforcement of the law and protection of civil liberties. After undergoing many changes in both houses of Congress, the Volstead Act—as the measure was known—became law. A lengthy and complicated document, it essentially provided the legal basis for the enforcement of the Eighteenth Amendment. It also provided

Minnesota representative Andrew J. Volstead helped draft the Volstead Act, which provided legal basis for the enforcement of the Eighteenth Amendment.

severe penalties; violators could receive fines ranging from $500 to $2,000 and up to five years in prison.

The Volstead Act also clearly states that "no person shall on or after the date when the eighteenth amendment to the Constitution of the United States goes into effect, manufacture, sell, barter, transport, import, export, deliver, furnish or possess any intoxicating liquor"[44] except in certain cases outlined in the new law. For example, Americans could obtain permits to acquire alcohol for industrial, medicinal, and even religious purposes. They were also allowed to produce limited amounts of wine and beer for personal consumption.

The new act, however, also defined an alcoholic beverage has having more than one-half of 1 percent alcohol. This provision surprised and angered many moderate Americans who had expected wine and beer, which had much lower alcohol content than hard liquor, to be exempt from prohibition.

The Volstead Act faced a political hurdle. President Wilson, who had always been unenthusiastic about prohibition, vetoed the new law on October 27. In his veto statement, Wilson said: "In all matters having to do with the personal habits and customs or large numbers of our people, we must be certain the established processes of legal change are followed."[45] Congress, however, quickly overrode his veto and made wartime prohibition permanent. That meant the long antialcohol struggle had ended. Whether prohibition would produce the social reform and moral improvement that thousands of temperance workers had hoped would be made clear soon after the Volstead Act took effect, at one minute after midnight, January 16, 1920.

Chapter Six

Prohibition Takes Effect

Millions of Americans cheered the coming of Prohibition. In their view, the long crusade to rid the country of a dangerous drug that caused death, dissolution, and despair had finally been achieved. Billy Sunday, the flamboyant revivalist preacher and exuberant supporter of Prohibition, spoke for many when he proclaimed, "Goodbye John [short for John Barleycorn, a nickname for liquor]. You were God's worst enemy. You were Hell's best friend.... The reign of tears is over."[46]

Many drys also thought that since the national government was enforcing Prohibition, their work was finished. They cheerfully predicted that once alcohol vanished from the marketplace, crime would drop, many prisons would close, families would become stronger, and the nation would be more united. Church bells pealed across the country to welcome the good news. Drys across America celebrated with ceremonies, public speeches, and noisy parades that featured actors dressed up as demons being run out of town.

Not everyone, of course, was pleased. The country's liquor industry was shocked. And so, too, were the millions of people who had fought the new ban. They faced the coming of Prohibition grim with anger and remorse. In the final hours before Prohibition became law, many bar owners draped their establishments in black and staged mock funerals for alcoholic drinks, as their customers drank their last lawful drinks.

The First Loophole

From the start of Prohibition, critics hoped and expected America's "Noble Experiment" to fail. Many brought attention to James Oglethorpe's futile attempt to ban alcohol in Georgia during the country's colonial period as proof that such laws are not effective. They also argued that drinking was a private matter

UNCLE SAM WILL *ENFORCE* PROHIBITION

BUY NOW!

This is the time to acquire your Wines and Liquors. Prices are advancing daily and will continue to advance whether Prohibition becomes effective July 1, 1919, or January 20, 1920. No Wines or Liquors may now be manufactured or imported—and existing stocks of good merchandise are almost extinct. Even if the ban on manufacture were lifted it would require years to mature the new product.

Specials This Week

	Per Case.	Per Bottle.
Imperial Gin	$24.50	$2.15
Dove Gin	27.00	2.30
Gordon Gin	29.00	2.45
Cocktail Rum (H. H. Dove Brand)	32.00	2.75
Bacardi Rum	37.00	3.20
Allash Kummel	30.00	2.60
Old Bridgeport Whiskey	36.00	3.10
(Six years old; bottled in bond)		
Green Creme de Menthe	34.00	3.00
(Imported in glass from Mouchotte Freres)		

Special inducements given to those buying Ports, Sherries, Clarets, Rhine and Moselle Wines in quantity.

HENRY HOLLANDER

Importers of Wines and Whiskies for the Connoisseur

ESTABLISHED 1877.

Telephone: Greeley 3218-3219 **149-151 West 36th St.** (Just West of B'way.)

Many Americans went on a shopping spree, buying as much alcohol as possible to store in their homes.

and could not be stamped out by government decree. Enforcement would also never work, they added, because the United States was too vast to patrol. In addition, they pointed out, there were too many loopholes in the law, and resourceful Americans who wanted to obtain alcohol would always find ways to do so.

In fact, the day before Prohibition officially went into effect, a federal judge ruled that law enforcement officials could legally confiscate any liquor found outside a private dwelling, such as in businesses and in vehicles. This news spurred many Americans to go on a shopping spree, buying up as much alcohol as possible to store in their homes. Bars quickly sold out their total supplies, as people hoarded wine, beer, and hard liquor. In private dwellings, many people believed, authorities would have more difficulty intruding upon privacy, unless they obtained search warrants from judges. This did not mean private stocks of liquor were safe, as many wealthy Americans later discovered when burglars broke into their homes and helped themselves to huge supplies of alcoholic beverages.

Prohibitionists Expect Compliance

Triumphant drys, however, predicted few enforcement problems. They insisted that the majority of Americans were law-abiding citizens who had obeyed government authority during World War I. Thus, they could be expected once again to do their patriotic duty and accept Prohibition.

One person who anticipated little trouble was John F. Kramer of Mansfield, Ohio, the first commissioner of the Prohibition Bureau—the federal government's newly created law enforcement agency. Kramer, in fact, suggested that enforcement costs would drop, as Americans became accustomed to Prohibition. But Kramer was wrong.

Enforcement Becomes a Problem

The federal government appropriated $6.5 million for the first year of enforcement. This was far too little. A few years later, Prohibition Bureau officials requested almost five times the original allocation to pay for the growing efforts to enforce Prohibition.

Following passage of the Volstead Act, state governments also passed their own prohibition enforcement laws, some of them stricter than federal law. But state lawmakers generally also did not adequately fund the new laws. All too soon, unexpected costs became clear. States had to hire not only more police officers, but also more judges, clerks, bailiffs, and other judicial system officials to keep up with the rising number of hearings and trials that clogged courtrooms. They also had to build more prisons and hire employees to run them.

Defying Prohibition

In response to growing expenses, many state officials backed away from enforcing Prohibition. Some argued that since the U.S. Congress took the lead in pushing for Prohibition, the federal government

Police hung posters but had a very difficult time enforcing Prohibition.

should assume most of the responsibility for enforcement, not the states.

As state and federal officials bickered, the number of Prohibition violations kept rising. Criminals were not the only violators. Otherwise law-abiding Americans also defied Prohibition. Many converted their garages and workshops into breweries and produced an estimated 700 million gallons of beer annually for commercial purposes.

Moonshine, Bathroom Gin, and Killer Concoctions

Americans also produced homemade wine in amounts that surpassed the legal limits. Meanwhile, thousands of makeshift distilleries large and small appeared in American forests and rural areas. Homegrown liquor producers set up stills in city apartments, basements, and the back rooms of stores and restaurants. Bathtubs in private homes served as preparation basins where amateur drink makers mixed glycerin, water, and juniper oil with alcohol to produce so-called bathroom gin, a popular drink in the Prohibition era. Various ethnic groups, such as Italians and Greeks, for instance, had enjoyed a long tradition of making wine, which they kept alive during Prohibition. The art of whisky-making was well-known to many Scots-Irish lineages in the Appalachian Mountains.

Moonshiners used stills like this to produce Tennessee whiskey for the black market during Prohibition.

Because many of these illegal whisky producers worked at night, distilling and smuggling distilled spirits to the black market, they earned the nickname of "moonshiner." Corrupt businessmen also sabotaged Prohibition by obtaining permits to purchase industrial-grade alcohol—which was still legal under the Volstead Act. Instead of using it for manufacturing purposes, as the law required, they used a variety of methods to convert the alcohol into drinkable beverages. To do this, illegal liquor makers had to filter out the poisons injected into the industrial alcohol to make it "denatured," or unfit, for consumption. Many of these concoctions were diluted with water and flavored with various ingredients in an attempt to make them taste like whisky or another liquor. Fancy, ornate labels were pasted on the bottles to deceive their customers into thinking they were buying genuine products. All too often, the filtering methods failed or were not used at all. As such, the processed beverages sickened, paralyzed, and killed thousands of drinking Americans.

During Prohibition, as many as fifteen thousand drinkers were stricken with a common malady known as jake foot. Those afflicted often lost total control of their feet from consuming drinks made from Jamaica ginger extract—which in some states contained denatured alcohol.

Even legitimate businesses found ways to skirt the law. Beer producers, for example, could still legally produce "near beer"—a grain-based beverage with less than one-half of 1 percent alcohol. The public, however, showed little interest in it. They wanted real beer.

Brewers quickly figured out how to satisfy that demand. They merely produced full strength beer as they always had and then neglected to draw off the alcohol to produce near beer, as the law required. As the brewers expected, understaffed and overworked government inspectors were seldom ever able to detect what was really in all those millions of beer bottles.

The demolition of near beer after Prohibition. Near beer was a legal grain-based beverage.

Whisky Prescriptions and Sacramental Wine

Even America's health professionals were corrupted by the new morality. Legions of doctors wrote prescriptions for themselves and friends to obtain dubious "medicines" that contained whisky—something permitted by the Volstead Act.

Some physicians even took bribes to write phony prescriptions for their patients. Druggists were also part of similar scams. Some obtained large amounts of medicinal alcohol from government warehouses, which they sold to neighborhood gangsters who peddled it on the black market.

Another loophole in the Volstead Act permitted religious institutions to obtain wine for sacramental purposes. Many Americans exploited this provision by hastily creating "churches" whose congregations were more interested in getting drunk than observing religious sacraments.

Americans also came up with a variety of ingenious ways to conceal their alcoholic beverages from scrutiny when they attended a dance, party, or public festival. Some hid their booze in thin flasks inside their sleeves or tied them to their belts. Others poured alcohol down hollow walking canes, capped them, and strapped canisters to one of their legs underneath a pair of trousers. Others hid flasks of whisky in their boots. Known as "bootlegging," this term was used to also describe trafficking in illegal alcohol.

Some Prohibition-era drinkers concealed the scent of alcohol by mixing liquor with other nonalcoholic, flavored beverages. Because the smell of gin was easy to cover up with other flavors, it was a popular liquor to use in mixed drinks in the 1920s.

Flouting the Law

Sometimes there was no attempt at secrecy. Fiorello La Guardia, a New York congressman and an avowed enemy of the Eighteenth Amendment, once gathered other lawmakers and journalists for a press conference in the House Office Building in Washington, D.C. Dressed as a bartender, the flamboyant lawmaker prepared legally obtained malt tonic to make an alcoholic drink that he happily drank, while reporters' cameras clicked.

La Guardia intended for his stunt to mock and flout Prohibition laws. Police at the scene, in fact, were so confused about whether the lawmaker had broken a law that they did nothing. Newspapers across the country carried the story. Soon groceries everywhere stocked their shelves with malt tonic, as Americans flocked to buy it.

Enterprising merchants also marketed other products that could be used to make alcoholic drinks. Various shops appeared everywhere that sold yeast, hops, and other ingredients and brewing apparatus needed for making beer at

Congressman Fiorello La Guardia brews his malt beer mix which was within the law—barely.

home. All this was legal, because the Volstead Act did not outlaw the sale or purchase of alcohol-making paraphernalia.

Even those individuals wanting to distill liquor had no problem buying special cookers and corn sugar mash, prepared for the home-whisky maker. Primitive distillation, in fact, was even possible with a teakettle and a simple towel.

Wine drinkers, meanwhile, could purchase blocks or bricks of compressed grape mixtures that could be dropped into a pitcher and mixed with water to turn them into grape juice that could then be converted into wine. Many big city department stores hired attractive young saleswomen to explain to their

Fiorella La Guardia
Protests Prohibition

Fiorella La Guardia, New York mayor, social activist, and U.S. congressman, testified against Prohibition during the 1926 Senate subcommittee hearings held to investigate the effects of Prohibition. La Guardia said,

> At least 1,000,000 quarts of liquor is consumed each day in the United States. In my opinion such an enormous traffic in liquor could not be carried on without the knowledge, if not the connivance [support] of the officials entrusted with the enforcement of the law....
>
> I believe that the percentage of whisky drinkers in the United States now is greater than in any other country of the world. Prohibition is responsible for that....
>
> At least $1,000,000,000 a year is lost to the National Government and the several States and counties in excise taxes. The liquor traffic is going on just the same. This amount goes into the pockets of bootleggers and in the pockets of the public officials in the shape of graft [payoffs]....
>
> It is my calculation that at least a million dollars a day is paid in graft and corruption to Federal, State, and local officers. Such a condition is not only intolerable, but it is demoralizing and dangerous to organized government....
>
> The drys seemingly are afraid of the truth.... Let us have an official survey and let the American people know what is going on. A complete and honest and impartial survey would reveal incredible conditions, corruption, crime, and an organized system of illicit traffic such as the world has never seen.

Quoted in U.S. Senate Committee on the Judiciary, *The National Prohibition Law*, 69th Cong., 1st sess., 1926, http://prohibition.osu.edu/content/laguardi.cfm.

customers the real intent of the product. The following series of "warnings" from a New York salesgirl in a Fifth Avenue store is typical of their approach:

Do not place the liquid in this jug and put it away in the cupboard for twenty-one days, because then it would turn into wine.

Do not stop the bottle with this cork containing this patented red rubber siphon hose, because that is necessary only when fermentation is going on.

Do not put the end of the tube into a glass of water, because that helps to make the fermenting liquor tasty and potable [drinkable].

Do not shake the bottle once a day, because that makes the liquor work.[47]

More Do-It-Yourself Products

As the do-it-yourself movement grew, savvy book publishers sold an assortment of how-to books to help readers make alcohol at home. Public libraries also provided the books for their patrons. In addition, Americans could turn to popular magazine articles to get ideas on how to make alcoholic drinks. Even the U.S. Department of Agriculture, which had provided information on home brewing before Prohibition, never stopped publishing brochures that explained how to create alcohol from a variety of foods, making these publications more popular than ever. The irony of the federal government providing this service during the Prohibition era is noted by author Eric Burns, who writes, "The same folks who had passed the law forbidding liquor were now providing detailed instructions on how to break it."[48]

The Criminal Element

The spirit of lawlessness in the 1920s grew as criminals entered the black market for alcoholic beverages. Smugglers,

The Words of a Rumrunner

In the following passage, an unidentified rumrunner recalls his work during hard times:

I was in the rum-running business for a couple of years, off and on. It was the only dollar you could make; they were only paying $35 to $40 a month in the three-masted coasters. I was in five schooners and some steamers that ran rum. They paid us in wages and bonus. A deck hand got $75 a month and $75 bonus. I was mate and got $150 a month and $150 bonus. The *Diamantina* was built in Lunenburg; she was a new vessel, had a crew of ten or 11, and would carry 6,000 cases. Really, they weren't cases; there were six bottles to a bag, sewed up in a diamond-shaped burlap package.... They used to get the liquor from Europe in wooden cases and they put the stuff in burlap there, because it was easier to stow and handle.... We had all kinds of customers.... The lobstermen would come out from Sheepshead Bay, and the scallopers, too. We used to sell small lots, as well as 600 to 800 cases to a boat. We took cash. Some of them came in speedboats.... We had rifles and so on aboard; I had a beautiful repeater shotgun.... There was an awful lot of graft going on with the characters, the hijacking, the police and the Coast Guard payoffs.

Quoted in Everett S. Allen, *The Black Ships: Rumrunners of Prohibition*, Boston, MA: Little, Brown, 1965, pp. 129–33.

for example, drove trucks loaded with bottles and kegs of liquor into the United States from Mexico and Canada. Sailing ships, nicknamed rumrunners, along with companion speedboats, hauled clandestine cargoes of liquor from the Bahamas, Cuba, and Europe to points of entry from New York to Florida. Smugglers were also busy along the Pacific coastline from Washington to California.

Now and then smugglers themselves became victims of other criminals on the high seas. Pirates often roamed the coasts, spying on the activities of smugglers. Suddenly, they would overtake rumrunners and hold up the crews at gunpoint, demanding the cash the smugglers had just received for their deliveries.

Criminals also sold alcohol at thousands of illegal bars, known as speakeasies that sprang up across the country. Patrons usually had to utter a password to gain entry into the hideaways, which ranged in quality from shabby backroom bars to fancy, expensive nightclubs that served dinner and featured jazz dance bands along with scantily dressed dancing girls who were hired to attract patrons.

A rum schooner impounded by police. Rumrunners brought illegal cargoes of liquor from the Bahamas and Cuba.

An Era of Organized Crime

Eventually organized crime took control of illegal alcohol business. In some places, it did this by sending out armed thugs who used intimidation and violence to extort payments of tribute from bootleggers, moonshiners, smugglers, and owners of speakeasies. Elsewhere, it set up its own operations. With millions of dollars in revenue at stake, rival gangs in America's big cities eventually collided. With submachine guns blazing, they fought over control of the liquor trade in various regions, especially when a crime syndicate tried to open operations in the territory of another. Gangsters bribed, threatened, beat, and killed anyone who got in their way, including police, Prohibition agents, and elected officials.

As these criminal enterprises expanded their operations, many adapted methods used by legitimate big businesses at the time. This meant they controlled all aspects of the illegal alcohol trade, including the production, transportation, and sale of the alcohol.

Law enforcement officials during the 1920s classified the gangs into two groups. Those in the rural areas and small towns of the West, Midwest, and the South were known as outlaws. They were generally native-born Americans who committed robbery, kidnapping, and murder. City gangsters, meanwhile, were called mobsters. These hoodlums

A New York Speakeasy

In the following excerpt, Paul Morand, a French author and diplomat, provides his impression in 1929 of a New York speakeasy bar:

They are usually situated downstairs and are identifiable by the large number of empty cars standing at their doors. The door is closed, and is only opened after you have been scrutinized through a door-catch or a barred opening. At night an electric torch suddenly gleams through a door-catch or a barred opening. At night an electric torch [flashlight] suddenly gleams through a pink silk curtain. There is a truly New York atmosphere of humbug [insincerity] in the whole thing. The interior is that of a criminal house; shutters are [closed] in full daylight, and one is caught in the smell of a cremation furnace for the ventilation is defective and grills are prepared under the mantelpieces of the fireplace.... The food is almost always poor, the service deplorable.... Yet, the speakeasy pervades Manhattan with a fascinating atmosphere of mystery. If only one could drink water there. Some speakeasies are disguised behind florists' shops, or behind undertakers' coffins. I know one, right in Broadway, which is entered through an imitation telephone-box.... [It is estimated that there are] 20,000 speakeasies in New York and it is unlikely that the police do not know them.

Quoted in David Colbert, ed., *Eyewitness to America: 500 Years of America in the Words of Those Who Saw It Happen*, New York: Pantheon, 1997, pp. 363–64.

were often immigrants or children of immigrants who took part in criminal organizations known as syndicates. City streets teemed with Irish, Jewish, and other ethnic gangs, but the most powerful and notorious were Italian mobsters, such as those of the Mafia.

The Reign of Al Capone

The most notorious Italian mobster was Al Capone, a corrupt, ruthless killer, whose rise during Prohibition came to symbolize the collapse of law and order in Chicago, Illinois. Born in Brooklyn, New York, Capone spent his youth as a petty criminal in a rough neighborhood. A knife gash to his face left him known for the rest of his life as Scarface.

After avoiding legal prosecution for killing two men, Capone moved to Chicago. Here, Scarface rose quickly to power in the city's underworld. By the late 1920s, Capone ran Chicago's most powerful crime syndicate and was responsible for operating a network of nightclubs, speakeasies, gambling operations, brothels, horse tracks, racetracks, distilleries, and breweries that brought in $60 million a year. He also commanded an army of about a thousand mobsters.

As ruthless and brutal as any warlord, Capone once reportedly killed a man with a baseball bat. Yet, he often displayed compassion for the city's homeless by contributing to charities, which earned him the reputation in some circles as a Robin Hood figure.

Brutal, shrewd, and cunning, Capone skillfully avoided arrests, political pressure, and revenge from his enemies in his armor-plated Cadillac. Although authorities could never prove his guilt, Capone was believed to have arranged the brutal murders of numerous rival gangsters.

The St. Valentine's Day Massacre

The most notorious of these killings took place in Chicago on Valentine's Day, 1929. Seven men stood in a cold city garage, waiting for a liquor delivery. They were members of a gang run by a mobster known as Bugs Moran, a Capone rival.

Suddenly, a car drove up. Out stepped five men, three dressed as police. Moran's men, possibly thinking this was a routine police raid, dropped their guns and lined up before a wall with their hands above their heads.

All at once, the two civilians accompanying the uniformed men brandished submachine guns and opened fire, riddling the captives with 150 bullets. Then the mobsters dressed as police pretended to arrest the gunmen and sped away in the car. It was all a murderous hoax.

The American people were outraged. Although gangland murders took the lives of about five hundred mobsters in Chicago alone during Prohibition, the St. Valentine's Day Massacre struck a public nerve. The bloody executions indicated a level of confidence and boldness that sent a shock wave throughout the country.

Suspicion for the killings fell immediately upon Capone. The mobster, as

Mob violence reached a new level with the St. Valentine's Day Massacre in Chicago on February 14, 1929.

usual, had an alibi; he was in Florida at the time of the slayings. Capone eventually did go to prison, but not for the vicious crimes he committed. Instead, federal prosecutors convicted him of tax evasion.

Chicago was hardly the only major American city infested with gangland violence. Vicious mobs also flourished in other big cities, such as New York, Kansas City, Miami, and Philadelphia. Americans became both fascinated and horrified with newspaper reports of gangsters and their criminal activities—which some historians think were sensationalized and exaggerated. They were also thrilled by accounts of Eliot Ness and his legendary band of incorruptible federal law enforcement agents—the Untouchables—who disrupted the crime activities of mobsters such as Capone.

Law Enforcement Problems

From its very beginning, however, the Prohibition Bureau quickly discovered that it lacked the resources to enforce the law adequately. It had funds for only 1,520 agents in 1920. During the next decade, the number of agents never exceeded 3,000, thus making it impossible for Prohibition agents to control the nation's 18,700-mile-long (30,095km)

A Federal Investigation

In February 1926, the vice president of the United States, Charles G. Dawes, representing the Better Government Association of Chicago and Cook County, presented Congress with a petition requesting an investigation of the lawlessness in the metropolitan area. The petition read in part:

> There has been for a long time in this city of Chicago a colony of unnaturalized persons, hostile to our institutions and laws, who have a formed a supergovernment of their own—feudists, black handers, members of the Mafia—who levy tribute upon citizens and enforce collections by terrorizing, kidnapping and assassinations....
>
> Many of these aliens have become fabulously rich as rum-runners and bootleggers, working in collusion with police and other officials, building up a monopoly in this unlawful business and dividing the territory of the county among themselves under penalty of death to all intruding competitors.
>
> Evidence multiplies daily that many public officials are in secret alliance with underworld assassins, gunmen, rum-runners, bootleggers, thugs, ballot box stuffers and repeaters, that a ring of politicians and public officials operating through criminals and with dummy directors are conducting a number of breweries and are selling beer under police protection, police officials, working out of the principal law enforcement office of the city, having been convoying liquor—namely alcohol, whisky and beer—and that one such police officer who is under Federal indictment is still acting as a police officer.

Quoted in John Kobler, *Capone: The Life and World of Al Capone*, New York: Da Capo, reprint 1992, pp. 166–67.

border. Nor did the bureau receive much enforcement help from the reluctant state governments. Ira L. Reeves, a federal Prohibition administrator in New York who quit his job in frustration, argued, "If we cannot trust our neighbors in our cities, in our counties, in our states, to enforce a law, then there can be no hope for its enforcement."[49]

Making matters worse, corruption was rampant in the criminal justice system. Numerous Prohibitions agents, along with policemen, Coast Guardsmen, judges, and political officials turned a blind eye to wrongdoings, after taking bribes from criminals. Fiorello La Guardia once joked that New York City alone would require a police force of

250,000 men and another force of 250,000 to "police the police."[50] An average of one of every twelve federal agents was fired annually for accepting bribes.

Izzy and Moe

Honest law-enforcement officials, however, made so many arrests that they overwhelmed the legal system. Isidor "Izzy" Einstein, and Moe Smith—two overweight, middle-aged, cigar-chomping, clownish Prohibition agents—made more than 4,932 arrests by themselves, 95 percent of which ended in conviction. In fact, they made 20 percent of all Prohibition arrests in New York during the years of Prohibition. Altogether, they seized 5 million bottles of alcohol and "busted" one hundred speakeasies a week in New York.

Austrian-born Izzy grew up on the tough streets on the East Side of New York, overweight and poorly educated. He was, however, cunning and resourceful as a Prohibition agent. For instance, one frigid, winter night, he stood outside a New York speakeasy in short sleeves until his flesh turned blue from the cold. Suddenly, Moe rushed his freezing partner inside and yelled, "Give this man a drink! He's just been bitten by a frost."[51] As a helpful bartender tried to assist,

Izzy and Moe seized five million bottles of alcohol in New York.

Moe seized the illegal bottle of alcohol and arrested him.

Izzy also had a knack for languages. By the time he became an agent, he was fluent in Hungarian, Polish, and German and had a working knowledge of several other languages by talking and listening to numerous immigrants in his neighborhood. Izzy put his linguistic ability and flair for disguise to work when he and Moe, a former cigar store owner, set out to catch Prohibition violators.

Using wigs, false moustaches, and false noses, Izzy and Moe showed up at speakeasies as grave diggers, streetcar conductors, concert musicians, Ivy League college boys, members of European royalty dressed in tuxedoes, and old ladies. Izzy even once impersonated a Chinese launderer and another time a Russian fisherman. On one occasion, the two undercover agents used black cork to darken their skin in an attempt to pass as African Americans wanting to buy illegal booze at a store in Harlem.

Most of their busts followed a similar pattern. After winning the confidence of those running the speakeasy, Izzy would announce, "Der's sad news here."[52] Then he and Moe would arrest everybody in the room.

By 1925 Izzy and Moe were known worldwide. Most likely it was their fame that led to their being fired that year. Jealousy from other agents may have played a role in having the well-known duo removed from their jobs. In addition, Izzy and Moe's supervisors became embarrassed over their antics. "The service must be dignified," a government spokesman suggested, while explaining the dismissal of the two men. "Izzy and Moe belong on the vaudeville stage [a form of popular entertainment]."[53] Amid a public outcry, Izzy and Moe departed the Prohibition agency and became salesmen.

Coping with Crowded Courts

Because of the high number of arrests during Prohibition—even though most lawbreakers were never apprehended— American courtrooms faced a backlog of cases. To keep up with them, many overworked judges took shortcuts in the legal process by setting up "bargain" days that allowed defendants to skip a trial, plead guilty, and avoid a stiff sentence. In addition, juries often showed their personal contempt for Prohibition laws by acquitting defendants that were probably guilty of trafficking in alcohol.

Such blatant miscarriages of justice in the courtroom, along with widespread criminal activity, the flouting of law by millions of otherwise law-abiding citizens, and the inability of law-enforcement officials to enforce Prohibition, all convinced a growing number of Americans that the Noble Experiment was a failure. And they wanted it stopped.

Chapter Seven

The Repeal of Prohibition

The case against Prohibition grew stronger with each passing day of the 1920s. Critics pointed out that the national ban on alcohol was supposed to reduce crime and corruption, improve social problems, lessen the number of prisons, and improve health and hygiene. When the Volstead Act first went into effect, liquor consumption went down 30 to 50 percent. Arrests for drunkenness also fell. However, as the anti-Prohibition forces found ways to get around law enforcement, these gains proved to be only temporary. In addition, the flouting of Prohibition merely bred contempt for other laws and encouraged antisocial, immoral, and sinful behavior. Crime had also become organized and therefore more of a menace to the country.

There were economic concerns too. Alcohol taxes had nearly vanished during Prohibition. Many Americans were angered that Prohibition had diverted millions of dollars from the regular economy into the hands of criminal thugs. And where, asked the critics, was any proof that business and industry saw an improvement in productivity or a reduction in absenteeism because workers were drinking less? They also claimed that any reduction in drinking was offset by an increase in taking drugs, such as marijuana.

By the end of the decade, a growing number of Americans were troubled by these objections and demanded that the nation take a second look at Prohibition.

President Hoover's Wickersham Commission

President Herbert Hoover, elected in 1928, agreed. His two predecessors, Warren G. Harding and Calvin Coolidge, had done little to address the negative consequences of Prohibition. Hoover, however, kept a campaign promise to appoint a high-level national commission, made up of respected educators, lawyers, and judges.

George Wickersham headed the Wickersham Commission, which analyzed the impact of the Eighteenth Amendment.

Prohibition and the Constitution

An amendment to the U.S. Constitution is more powerful than a law, which is why the advocates of temperance fought for passage of the Eighteenth Amendment, which, in addition to congressional approval, had to be ratified by three-fourths of the states. The only way to undo an amendment is another amendment, which in the case of the Prohibition was the Twenty-First Amendment. The text of both amendments is below.

Amendment XVIII

Section 1. After one year from the ratification of this article the manufacture, sale, or transportation of intoxicating liquors within, the importation thereof into, or the exportation thereof from the United States and all territory subject to the jurisdiction thereof for beverage purposes is hereby prohibited.

Section 2. The Congress and the several states shall have concurrent power to enforce this article by appropriate legislation.

Section 3. This article shall be inoperative unless it shall have been ratified as an amendment to the Constitution by the legislatures of the several states, as provided in the Constitution, within seven years from the date of the submission hereof to the states by the Congress.

Amendment XXI

Section 1. The eighteenth article of amendment to the Constitution of the United States is hereby repealed.

Section 2. The transportation or importation into any state, territory, or possession of the United States for delivery or use therein of intoxicating liquors, in violation of the laws thereof, is hereby prohibited.

Section 3. This article shall be inoperative unless it shall have been ratified as an amendment to the Constitution by conventions in the several states, as provided in the Constitution, within seven years from the date of the submission hereof to the states by the Congress.

Source: Cornell University Law School, www.law.cornell.edu/constitution/constitution.table .html#amendments.

Headed by George W. Wickersham, a highly respected barrister, the commission spent nineteen months and a half-million dollars analyzing the impact of the Eighteenth Amendment. The commission conducted several public hearings, during which it collected testimonies and data from a wide range of supporters and critics of Prohibition.

Hopes ran high across the country that the Wickersham Commission would help Americans to understand whether its Noble Experiment was working. However, when the commission finally published its findings, it managed to disappoint both sides of the controversy. The report provided analysis and plenty of data, but the commission took no sides on the issue and made no definitive recommendations. Drys and wets both condemned the committee's work.

Nonetheless, the word *repeal* gained popularity. More and more Americans confessed to strong misgivings about Prohibition and wanted the law repealed, or at least modified to make wine and beer legal.

Organized Resistance to Prohibition

Long before the Wickersham Commission issued its report, a national protest movement against Prohibition was underway. It was led by a new organization, the Association Against the Prohibition Amendment (AAPA). The nation's first wet anti-Prohibition organization was founded in 1920 by William H. Stayton, a former naval officer and lawyer, who recruited professionals, university leaders, judges, military leaders, elected officials, and businessmen opposed to Prohibition on the grounds that government did not have the authority to criminalize personal liberty. These respected and influential individuals were hard for drys to dismiss.

Thanks in part to the work of the AAPA, the tide of public opinion began to change. Adopting some of the same methods used by the Anti-Saloon League, Stayton's organization raised vast sums of money to support wet candidates. It kept track of the voting record of Congress on Prohibition measures and funded propaganda in the form of articles and research studies that favored claims that Prohibition had failed. Unlike the league, however, the AAPA employed the talents of advertising professionals who ran a slick public relations campaign.

One of its tactics was to exaggerate the connection between Prohibition and crime. Another was to satirize drys as blue-nosed Puritans who were opposed to life's pleasures. Drinking alcohol, their propaganda suggested, was normal and respectable. Alcohol could be good for the country as well. For example, it could serve as an alternative fuel for automobiles. AAPA also wanted to be seen by the public as being reasonable. The letterhead on the organization's stationery stated, "Beer and Light Wines NOW; But No Saloons EVER."[54]

Businesses Supporting Repeal

The AAPA also had powerful allies. Devastated by Prohibition, the beer, wine, and liquor industries were fighting to regain their lost business. Even some bootleggers supported repeal, assuming that they could add customers if drinking were made lawful. Other businesses lent support. Among them were those with economic self-interests.

Business tycoon Pierre Du Pont spoke for many wealthy businessmen in 1932 when he pointed out during a radio talk show that "the income tax would not be necessary in the future and half the revenue required for the [federal government's] budget ... would be furnished by the tax on liquor alone."[55]

Some business leaders, however, simply thought that Prohibition had not lived up to expectations. For example, John D. Rockefeller, the oil-refining titan and a teetotaler, had once given financial support to the Anti-Saloon League. However, he now said, "It is my profound conviction that the benefits of the Eighteenth Amendment are more than outweighed by the evils that have developed and flourished since its adoption."[56]

Organizations Supporting Repeal

There were also other organizations that joined the repeal movement. One of them was the Women's Organization for National Prohibition Reform (WONPR). Begun in May 1929 by Pauline H. Sabin,

Members from the Women's Organization for National Prohibition Reform inviting people to join their anti-Prohibition club.

the wife of a well-known New York banker, the group attracted a million members within two years. The WONPR did not advocate a return of saloons, but it wanted Prohibition to come to an end. Its mission statement read, "We are convinced that National Prohibition, wrong in principle, has been equally disastrous in consequences in the hypocrisy, the corruption, the tragic loss of life and the appalling increase of crime which have attended the abortive attempt to enforce it."[57]

The American Bar Association—the professional organization for attorneys—also came out against Prohibition. It was joined by the American Federation of Labor, the nation's largest labor union.

Much of the news media also took aim at the Eighteenth Amendment. Many big city newspapers that had once played a big role in supporting the crusade to ban alcohol now featured editorials in favor of doing away with, or weakening, Prohibition. Small-town papers, which were more likely to support Prohibition, were disappearing as their readers relocated to the nation's big cities in search of new jobs.

In addition, many intellectuals, artists, and journalists in big cities, such as New York, undertook a campaign to ridicule and criticize Prohibition and its supporters. Their works often portrayed America's antialcohol legions as small-minded, prudish, old-fashioned opponents of personal liberty. They suggested that such attitudes also led to suppression of free expression of art and literature. H.L. Mencken, a Baltimore journalist and fierce social critic, even resorted to name-calling, as seen in this diatribe:

> It was among country Methodists, practitioners of a theology [religious belief] degraded to the level of voodooism, that Prohibition was invented.... [The foundation of this belief] ... is the yokel's congenital [inborn] and incurable hatred of the city man—his simian [apelike] rage against anyone who, as he sees it, is having a better time than he is.[58]

A powerful new medium—the motion picture—also pushed the repeal agenda. By the end of the decade, an estimated 110 million Americans went to movie theaters every week. Many of these films depicted heroes drinking bootleg alcohol in a positive light. Comedies, meanwhile, often ridiculed supporters of Prohibition as being hopelessly pious and narrow-minded busybodies. Motion pictures also glamorized romance and sex, which may have helped to undermine traditional beliefs. Breaking taboos, which included drinking illicit liquor, became a norm for millions of postwar young Americans that Prohibition-era author F. Scott Fitzgerald called the "Lost Generation."

A Shift in Traditional Values

The rise of popular support for repeal revealed a shift in values in American society. The 1920s, in fact, was a decade typified by a clash between traditionalists and proponents of the modern.

Younger Americans were more open to social taboos, such as drinking and smoking.

Many of the nation's older, more deeply rooted values and beliefs of thrift, hard work, and godliness had been nurtured by centuries of traditional, Christian teachings and rural and small-town life.

In contrast to these were values and beliefs born of a new, modern, technology-based, way of life. Social scientist John C. Burnham believes there is clear evidence to show that "ideas of dominant groups of Americans about what was acceptable and respectable began to turn upside down as the campaign to undermine Prohibition gathered momentum."[59]

This inversion of values was common among many young people. It was especially apparent in America's urban areas, where younger generations of Americans were more likely to tolerate, or even violate, social taboos, such as drinking, smoking, cursing, and having sex outside of marriage.

World War I also led people to reconsider traditional ideas of right and wrong. During the war, many uniformed American young men adopted "tough-guy" behaviors by drinking, smoking, cursing, and playing cards. When the war ended, many veterans continued these behaviors in civilian society. They, along with many others in their generation, also were disillusioned by World War I. The catastrophe created by the dark side of human nature convinced millions of young Americans that they should lead their lives in pursuit of pleasure and rule-breaking before the next man-made tragedy befell them.

Other forces disturbed the social order during the 1920s. Automobiles, for the first time, became common on the nation's highways and gave millions of Americans a new freedom. In addition, labor-saving devices, such as vacuum cleaners, washing machines, and refrigerators freed women from much of the drudgery of domestic housework, allowing them to pursue other interests. Traditional restrictions placed on women started to lessen. During the 1920s, many fashionable and rebellious young women, known as "flappers," made a point of shocking their elders by smoking and drinking in public. Meanwhile, revolutionary ideas about human psychology, evolution, communism, and time and space challenged traditional biblical teachings, thus weakening the authority of many ministers, who relied on holy scripture to condemn drinking and drinkers. Jazz music, with its emphasis on breaking the rules of music, became the anthem of the 1920s. All of these changes helped push rules of society to the limit. Small wonder that the decade of Prohibition has been labeled both "the Roaring 20s" and the "Lawless Decade."

Economic Forces Work Against Prohibition

Economic concerns also took a toll on Prohibition. Much of the 1920s had been a prosperous time for most Americans. Much of the wealth they enjoyed came from investing in a rising stock market, often using borrowed money. But in October 1929, the stock markets crashed, as panicked Americans sold their shares before they dropped most of their value or became worthless. Next, thousands of businesses and banks collapsed, as millions of Americans lost their savings and their jobs.

The Depression caused many to feel that eliminating Prohibition would help the country's economy by putting millions of people back to work in alcohol-related industries.

By the early 1930s, it was clear that the United States, along with nations around the world, had sunk into a catastrophic economic depression. All at once the nation's capitalistic economic system—once considered the mightiest in the world—had failed and showed no signs of immediate recovery. Millions of Americans now looked to the federal government for help. Legions of the unemployed also believed that the Eighteenth Amendment had deprived the government of millions of dollars in tax revenues that could now be used to aid suffering Americans. Critics argued that ridding the nation of Prohibition would put millions of people back to work in distilleries, breweries, transportation, and retail. "Money had a lot to do with the change in the nation's attitude toward prohibition—money rather than morals,"[60] observes author Donald Barr Chidsey.

Defending Prohibition in Tough Times

Staunch enemies of alcohol, however, defended Prohibition, believing it had done its job. They also were convinced that a social movement—despite its shortcomings—that took nearly a century to reach its goal was now deeply entrenched in American society. Moreover, a campaign to repeal a constitutional amendment seemed to many people to be an impossible undertaking. At least, it had never been done before. "There is as much chance of repealing the Eighteenth Amendment as there is for a hummingbird to fly to the planet Mars with the Washington Monument tied to its tail,"[61] observed U.S. senator Morris Sheppard of Texas in September 1930.

Prohibition's apologists, however, were losing energy, revenue, legitimacy, and public support. For one thing, ever since accomplishing their goal, the nation's major dry Prohibition organizations, such as the Anti-Saloon League, had difficulty keeping their members excited and supportive of Prohibition. Membership and contributions declined after the Volstead Act went into effect. When the Depression came, financial support dropped even more. Gone, too, were the intense crusading spirit and sense of purpose that once united millions of dry Americans. They were exhausted.

Worse yet for prohibitionists, the Anti-Saloon League's effective, brilliant leader, Wayne B. Wheeler, died in 1927. His health had been failing ever since his wife died in a tragic kitchen fire a few years before. Her father, a friend of Wheeler's, also died from a heart attack after witnessing his daughter's death.

Wheeler's successor was James Cannon Jr., a bishop in the Methodist Episcopal Church in the South. A stern, conservative man, Cannon also had a strong puritanical streak that went beyond supporting Prohibition. He railed not only against drinking alcohol, but also against playing cards, consuming soft drinks, and taking walks on Sunday. He lacked, however, the leadership skills and authority to motivate millions of drys. All these changes weakened the league and made it incapable of competing with the better-organized, well-funded, and committed AAPA.

National polls indicated a growing public support for repeal that alarmed prohibitionists. In 1930 the *Literary Digest*, a popular weekly magazine, conducted a national survey that revealed that majorities in all but five states favored repealing Prohibition. In addition, a poll taken by the Newspaper Enterprise Association in forty-seven states showed that almost half of the respondents wanted Prohibition to be weakened, and 31.3 percent wanted repeal.

The End of Prohibition

Sensing the new national sentiment, many politicians changed course too. In the 1932 presidential election, many Republicans favored giving the states the option of deciding for themselves whether to legalize liquor. In contrast, the Democratic Party and its candidate, Franklin Delano Roosevelt, made it clear they favored repeal of Prohibition at the national level. Democrats took control of Congress in 1933 and quickly passed a bill authorizing the Twenty-First Amendment that would repeal the Eighteenth Amendment. The measure was next transmitted to the states for ratification.

Action came quickly. By December 5, 1933, three-fourths of the states had approved the new amendment. National prohibition was dead. That evening newly elected President Roosevelt issued a proclamation declaring that alcoholic beverages were again legal. He added,

The Twenty-First Amendment ended Prohibition in 1933.

I ask the wholehearted cooperation of all our citizens to the end that this return of individual freedom shall not be accompanied by the repugnant conditions that obtained prior to the adoption of the 18th Amendment and those that have existed since its adoption. Failure to do this honestly and courageously will be a living reproach to us all. I ask especially that no State shall by law or otherwise authorize the return of the saloon either in its old form or in some modern guise.[62]

Aftermath of Repeal

For better or worse, America's thirteen-year ban on alcohol left America a changed nation. Contrary to the claims of some wet critics, alcohol consumption did not rise during the years of Prohibition.

Studies, in fact, showed that average consumption per person during the entire 1920s may have dropped by as much as 50 percent from a decade earlier. Furthermore, alcohol consumption remained at a reduced level for several decades following repeal. That also meant a drop in related health and medical problems.

The Twenty-First Amendment did not totally repeal all bans on drinking. Prohibition, in fact, remained in some counties and states for decades, thanks to section two of the amendment which reads, "The transportation or importation into any State, Territory, or possession of the United States for delivery or use therein of intoxicating liquors, in violation of the laws thereof, is hereby prohibited." The wording of this passage was intended to allow those states wishing to remain dry to reject shipments of alcohol from wet states.

A bartender serves the first beers after Prohibition.

Despite the passage of the Twenty-First Amendment, a widespread fear of Prohibition's return haunted many Americans for decades after repeal took effect. Knowing well how changing economic and moral concerns could shut down businesses and industries, many in the liquor industry remained vigilant for signs of any renewed interest in Prohibition. They were quick to launch propaganda attacks against writers and professors who spoke out against alcohol. Local governments that dared to let citizens vote on new temperance could also count on facing the wrath of the liquor interests.

Drys also were angry for many years. Some bitter supporters of Prohibition remained convinced that powerful businessmen immorally used their wealth and influence to lead the nation away from Prohibition merely for their own economic benefit. "By comparison with this, Judas Iscariot, who sold his Lord for thirty pieces of silver, was a mere unsophisticated novice and Benedict Arnold was a loyal patriot,"[63] complained George B. Cutten, president of New York's Colgate University, in his 1944 book, *Should Prohibition Return?*

A fascination with gangsters became a lasting fixture in American life. Many films and novels glorified mobsters and gangsters. Organized crime, which began during Prohibition, continues to haunt Americans, as dangerous mobs battle over drug trafficking in modern times.

Finally the repeal of America's Noble Experiment continues to play a role in modern debates about other social ills. Many Americans wonder: If the federal government can no longer restrain adult consumption of alcohol, why does it then have the right to try to curb other social ills, such prostitution, gambling, and the use of illicit drugs, such as marijuana and cocaine? One thing is clear: Those who consider these issues have a rich and complex history of temperance, prohibition, and repeal to guide them.

Notes

Introduction: The Noble Experiment

1. Quoted in Dennis Nishi, ed., *Prohibition*, San Diego, CA: Greenhaven Press, 2003, p. 75.

Chapter One: The Origins of Alcohol Abuse in America

2. Eric Burns, *The Spirits of America: A Social History of Alcohol*, Philadelphia, PA: Temple University Press, 2004, p. 18.
3. Burns, *The Spirits of America*, p. 17.
4. Quoted in Anne Boyd, "Reform Movements: Temperance," *American Eras*, 1997, on Encyclopedia.com. www.encyclopedia.com/doc/1G2-2536601057.html.
5. Quoted in Burns, *The Spirits of America*, p. 47.
6. Quoted in Ben Jankowski, "The Making of Prohibition Part I: The History of Political and Social Forces at Work for Prohibition in America," *Brewing Techniques*, November–December 1994, www.brewingtechniques.com/library/backissues/issue2.6/jankowski.html.
7. Quoted in Daniel J. Boorstin, *The Americans: The Colonial Experience*, New York: Random House, 1958, p. 82.
8. Boorstin, *The Americans*, p. 91.
9. Quoted in Edward Behr, *Prohibition: Thirteen Years That Changed America*, New York: Arcade, 1996, p. 14.
10. W.J. Rorabaugh, *The Alcoholic Republic: An American Tradition*, New York: Oxford University Press, 1979, p. 151.
11. Rorabaugh, *The Alcoholic Republic*, p. xi.
12. Quoted in Steve Simon, "Alexander Hamilton and the Whiskey Tax," Washington, DC: Alcohol and Tobacco Tax and Trade Bureau, U.S. Department of the Treasury, www.ttb.gov/public_info/special_feature.shtml.

Chapter Two: The Temperance Movement Begins

13. Quoted in Behr, *Prohibition*, p. 17.
14. Quoted in Rorabaugh, *The Alcoholic Republic*, p. 43.
15. Quoted in J.C. Furnas, *The Americans: A Social History of the United States 1587–1914*, New York: Putnam's, 1969, p. 503.
16. Burns, *The Spirits of America*, p. 81.
17. Lyman Beecher, *Six Sermons on the Nature, Occasions, Signs, Evils, and Remedy of Intemperance*, Boston, MA: Marvin, 1828, www.iath.virginia.edu/utc/sentimnt/sneslbat.html.
18. Quoted in J.C. Furnas, *The Life and Times of the Late Demon Rum*, New York: Capricorn, 1965, p. 82.
19. Quoted in Behr, *Prohibition*, p. 24.
20. Quoted in Behr, *Prohibition*, p. 25.
21. Quoted in Furnas, *The Life and Times of the Late Demon Rum*, p. 52.

22. Quoted in Behr, *Prohibition*, p. 22.
23. Lorenzo D. Johnson, *Martha Washingtonianism, Or a History of the Ladies' Temperance Benevolent Societies*, New York: Saxton, 1843, www.teachushistory.org/second-great-awakening-age-reform/resources/womens-temperance-society-history.
24. Furnas, *The Americans*, pp. 508–509.
25. Quoted in Will Bartlett, "A History of Alcohol," Blethan Maine Newspapers, October 19, 1997, http://pressherald.mainetoday.com/specialrpts/alcohol/d1hist.htm.
26. Quoted in Bartlett "A History of Alcohol."
27. Quoted in Furnas, *The Americans*, p. 512.
28. Charles Taber Stout, "Lincoln on Prohibition: Quotes from Legislature to Show Lincoln's Opposition: April 8, 1922, Saturday page 12," *New York Times*, http://query.nytimes.com/gst/abstract.html?res=9E07E6D61639EF3ABC4053DFB2668389639EDE.
29. Burns, *The Spirits of America*, p. 94.

Chapter Three: Women's Crusade Against Demon Rum

30. Carol Mattingly, *Well-Tempered Women: Nineteenth-Century Temperance Rhetoric*, Carbondale: Southern Illinois University Press, 1998, p. 14.
31. Quoted in Mattingly, *Well-Tempered Women*, p. 23.
32. Mattingly, *Well-Tempered Women*, p. 42.
33. Quoted in Mattingly, *Well-Tempered Women*, p. 26.
34. Quoted in Mattingly, *Well-Tempered Women*, p. 60.

Chapter Four: The Anti-Saloon Campaign Takes Charge

35. Donald Barr Chidsey, *On and Off the Wagon: A Sober Analysis of the Temperance Movement from the Pilgrims Through Prohibition*, New York: Cowles, 1969, p. 2.
36. Quoted in Robert Garrett, "Saving Their Husbands, One Saloon at a Time," CityPulse, July, 5, 2006, www.lansingcitypulse.com/lansing/article-302-saving-their-husbands-one-saloon-at-a-time.html.
37. Quoted in Edward Griffith, *Alcohol: The World's Favorite Drug*, New York: St. Martin's, 2003, p. 101.
38. Quoted in Griffith, *Alcohol*, p. 102.
39. Carry A. Nation, *The Use and Need of the Life of Carry A. Nation*, Topeka, KS: Steves & Sons, 1908, www.kshs.org/exhibits/carry/smashing.htm.
40. Quoted in PBS, "Carrie Nation," PBS, www.pbs.org/wgbh/amex/1900/peopleevents/pande4.html.
41. Quoted in David Colbert, ed., *Eyewitness to America: 500 Years of America in the Words of Those Who Saw It Happen*, New York: Pantheon, 1997, p. 310.
42. Quoted in Mattingly, *Well-Tempered Women*, p. 176.
43. Quoted in Burns, *The Spirits of America*, p. 145.

Chapter Five: Setting the Stage for National Prohibition

44. Historycentral.com, "Volstead Act 1920," Historycentral.com, www.historycentral.com/documents/Volstead.html.
45. Quoted in Richard Mendelson, *From Demon to Darling: A Legal History of Wine in America*, Berkeley: University of California Press: 2009, p. 61.

Chapter Six: Prohibition Takes Effect

46. Quoted in Ernest R. May, *War, Boom and Bust 1917–1932*, vol. 10, *The Life History of the United States*, ed., Henry H. Graff, New York: Time, 1964, p. 46.

47. Quoted in Robert Maddox, "The War Against Demon Rum," *American History Volume 2: Reconstruction Through the Present*, ed. Robert Maddox, Guilford: CT: Dushkin, 1989, p. 103.

48. Burns, *The Spirits of America*, p. 194.

49. Quoted in Nishi, *Prohibition*, p. 186.

50. Quoted in Maddox, "The War Against Demon Rum," p. 102.

51. Quoted in Bill Lawrence, *Fascinating Facts from American History*, Portland, ME: Walch, 1995, p. 167.

52. Quoted in Jay Maeder, "Rumhounds Izzy & Moe," December 23, 2001, *Daily News*, www.nydailynews.com/archives/news/2001/12/23/2001-12-23_rumhounds_izzy___moe.html.

53. Quoted in Burns, *The Spirits of America*, p. 245.

Chapter Seven: The Repeal of Prohibition

54. Quoted in John C. Burnham, *Bad Habits: Drinking, Smoking, Taking Drugs, Gambling, Sexual Misbehavior and Swearing in American History*, New York: New York University Press, 1994, p. 433.

55. Quoted in Burnham, *Bad Habits*, p. 46.

56. Quoted in Jean Edward Smith, *FDR*, New York: Random House, 2007, p. 267.

57. Excerpt from WONPR Convention, April 23–24, 1939, *Women's Organization for National Prohibition Reform*. www.wonpr.org/history.htm.

58. Quoted in Burnham, *Bad Habits*, p. 36.

59. Burnham, *Bad Habits*, p. 24.

60. Chidsey, *On and Off the Wagon*, p. 128.

61. Quoted in Chidsey, *On and Off the Wagon*, p. 127.

62. Franklin D. Roosevelt, "187–Proclamation 2065–Repeal of the Eighteenth Amendment," December 5, 1933, American Presidency Project, www.presidency.ucsb.edu/ws/index.php?pid=14570.

63. Quoted in Nishi, *Prohibition*, p. 209.

For More Information

Books

Suzanne Lieurance, *The Prohibition Era in American History*. Berkeley Heights, NJ: Enslow, 2003. A concise history of the temperance movement and Prohibition.

Eileen Lucas, *The Eighteenth and Twenty-First Amendments: Alcohol, Prohibition, and Repeal*. Berkeley Heights, NJ: Enslow, 1998. An informative look at Prohibition.

Bill Severn, *The End of the Roaring Twenties: Prohibition and Repeal*. New York: Julian Messner, 1965. A well-written, fact-filled account of the rise of the temperance and Prohibition movements.

Diane Yancey, *Al Capone*. San Diego, CA: Lucent Books, 2003. An informative, well-illustrated biography of a notorious mobster.

Web Sites

Lost Museum (http://chnm.gmu.edu/lostmuseum/searchlm.php?function=find&exhibit=temperance&browse=temperance). Among other historical topics this site features primary sources for the temperance movement created by the New Media Lab at City University of New York's Graduate School.

Pictorial Americana: Selected Images from the Collection of the Library of Congress (http://www.loc.gov/rr/print/list/picamer/paTemper.html). This Library of Congress site contains historical images of original drawings, paintings, and other images that depict various characters and themes of the temperance movement.

Temperance & Prohibition (www.prohibition.osu.edu). An excellent online source from Ohio State University offering primary sources.

Index

Picture Credits

Cover: Time Life Pictures/National Archives/Time Life Pictures/Getty Images

AP Images, 9 (bottom left and middle), 60, 98, 100

© Bettmann/Corbis, 25, 30, 32, 55, 56, 63, 79, 80, 83, 86, 94

© BWAC Images/Alamy, 78

© Corbis, 12, 42, 48, 53, 69, 71, 72, 91

Hulton Archive/Getty Images, 38, 65

Illustrated London News/Getty Images, 8 (bottom right)

Kean Collection/Hulton Archive/Getty Images, 23

Marc Charmet/The Art Archive/The Picture Desk, Inc., 8 (upper left)

© Minnesota Historical Society/ Corbis, 101

MPI/Getty Images, 20, 46

© North Wind Picture Archives/ Alamy, 17

Public Domain, 28, 75

The Library of Congress, 9 (upper right), 11, 34, 40, 96

© The London Art Archive/Alamy, 15

Topical Press Agency/Hulton Archive/ Getty Images, 50

© Underwood & Underwood/Corbis, 77, 88

About the Author

John M. Dunn is a freelance writer and high school history teacher. He has taught in Georgia, Florida, North Carolina, and Germany. As a writer and journalist, he has published numerous articles and stories in more than 20 periodicals, as well as scripts for audio-visual productions and a children's play. His books *The Russian Revolution*, *The Relocation of the North American Indian*, *The Spread of Islam*, *Advertising*, *The Civil Rights Movement*, *The Enlightenment*, *Life During the Black Death*, *The Vietnam War: A History of U.S. Involvement*, *The Computer Revolution*, *The French Revolution: The Fall of the Monarchy*, and *Life in Castro's Cuba*, are published by Lucent Books. He lives with his wife and two daughters in Ocala, Florida.